George Q. Cannon

HIS MISSIONARY YEARS

George Q. Cannon

HIS MISSIONARY YEARS

Lawrence R. Flake

Bookcraft
Salt Lake City, Utah

This book is dedicated to our eight children—
especially Cannon William Flake

Library of Congress Catalog Card Number 98-74301
ISBN 1-57008-561-7

First Printing, 1998

Printed in the United States of America

CONTENTS

CHAPTER I

Introduction

During the second week of April, 1901, nearly every prominent newspaper in the United States and many foreign papers chronicled the passing of George Quayle Cannon.[1] One newspaper called him "the Mormon Richelieu," who "ranks next after Joseph Smith and Brigham Young among the builders of the Mormon Church."[2] The accomplishments of his seventy-four-year lifetime are numerous and impressive:

—Member of the First Presidency of The Church of Jesus Christ of Latter-day Saints for a quarter of a century, serving as counselor to four presidents[3]

—Missionary of the Church for fifteen years, serving five missions and traveling more than thirty thousand miles

George Q. Cannon, ca. 1855

—Superintendent of the Deseret Sunday School Union for thirty-four years, membership 120,000[4] at his death

—Millionaire business and industrial magnate

—Polygamist, husband of five wives and father of thirty-five children

—Chancellor of the University of Deseret for ten years

—Prolific editor, publisher, and author of newspapers, magazines, and books

—Utah Territory's representative to Congress for five terms

—Apostle of the Lord Jesus Christ for forty years

The San Francisco Examiner reported, "George Q. Cannon, one of the most widely known men in America, banker, statesman, politician, missionary, railroad director, apostle and the recognized brains of the Mormon Church, is no more."[5] And the *Idaho Daily Statesman* asserted: "The death of George Q. Cannon removes one of the remarkable men of the intermountain country. He was a leader—a man of great ability and powerful influence. For many years he has been recognized as the real head of the Mormon Church, and his death will be a great loss to the organization."[6]

Even those papers that considered Mormonism a threat recognized the power of George Q. Cannon: "He was next in line for the presidency of the church, and had he lived to take that office, he would have been a dangerous man."[7]

In a tribute paid to President Cannon, fellow Apostle Heber J. Grant related this incident: "When a number of leading statesmen were discussing different men and were endeavoring to decide as to who were the eight brightest minds in America, President Cannon's name was one of the eight."[8] He was prominent not only in America but also in Europe, where he had served as a mission president. "At the close of 1901, the year of his death, the show windows of the celebrated commercial emporium of the most noted Avenue in Berlin, Germany, the magnificent Unter den Linden, displayed his portrait along with six others, as the principal world personalities whom death had taken during the previous twelve months. His seat was undisputedly among the mighty."[9]

Orson F. Whitney, an eminent Utah historian and personal friend of George Q. Cannon, gave this lofty evaluation:

> His forte, in secular affairs, was statecraft, and in the field of diplomacy, Utah, among all her gifted sons, has not seen his equal. Much of the prestige he possessed was undoubtedly due to his ecclesiastical prominence; but it was not office that gave him intellect, eloquency, magnetism, and all those rare qualities which enabled him to mould and sway the minds and heart of men. He would have been a man of mark in any community. Had he remained in his native England, he would probably have been heard of in Parliament, and it is within the bounds of conservative calculation to imagine such a one the peer of Gladstone, Disraeli and other premiers of the realm.[10]

Because President Cannon's accomplishments cover so many vast fields, as the list above indicates, a comprehensive study of his life would comprise many volumes. The index to the Journal History of the Church alone contains approximately 2,500 references to him. He wrote more than a thousand editorials for his publication, *The Juvenile Instructor,* and served many years as a newspaper editor. More than three hundred of his discourses have been published, and the total number of words in the books and articles he has written has been estimated at over two million.[11] President Heber J. Grant wrote, "The record made by

him in writing [alone] is a great one, equalled by but few who
have devoted their entire life to literary pursuits."[12] His contribution to the Latter-day Saint Sunday School would alone fill a
volume. In regard to this one achievement, one writer postulated
that if George Q. Cannon

> had performed no other work in life than that which he has ac-
> complished in connection with the Sunday School cause, it would
> entitle him to have his name handed down as a benefactor, to the
> latest generation. What he has produced under the blessing of
> God, through this agency, radiates beyond the limits of time and
> stretches into eternity, where the multiplication of its effects will
> parallel duration.[13]

Further, President Cannon was known throughout the
Church and in the Congress of the United States as a powerful
public speaker. One listener attested to his prowess in this area:
"On Sund. Elder Geo. Q. Cannon delivered one of the Most
Heavenly and Angelic discourses that I ever heard in My Life on
the order of Enoch. His remarks were so forcible and Powerful
that one almost imagined himself the vision of the mind before
them, as I had whilest listening to the Discourse, they would live
so as to be worthy to enter therein."[14]

His contribution to higher education included service to the
University of Deseret (University of Utah) and Brigham Young
Academy (Brigham Young University). Heber J. Grant noted:
"There has been no other man in Utah who has shown such
marked ability in so many different ways as he has. The broad
educational views held by President Cannon entitle him to be
ranked as one of the foremost men, from an educational stand-
point, that Utah has ever produced."[15]

His many years of service as an Apostle, and especially his service as a Counselor to four Presidents of the Church caused many people to consider him more influential than the three Presidents who succeeded Brigham Young. *The Boston Globe* declared: "The death of George Q. Cannon removes from the sphere of worldly activities a Mormon leader who was second in power and influence only to that born ruler, Brigham Young himself."[16] His life history parallels the history of the Church itself for more than five decades: "The precision with which the personal history of George Q. Cannon fits into the historical superstructure of the Church, constituting, as it does, an indispensable portion of it, proves that his place and part in its affairs were predetermined by the Designer, who foreordained the destiny of both."[17]

The foundation for true greatness is almost invariably laid in the formative years of youth, and so it was with George Q. Cannon. The outstanding literary, political, executive, and spiritual powers that made him a great and famous man all emerged during the fifteen-year missionary period of his early life. This book will include his first thirty-seven years, consisting of his boyhood in Liverpool and Nauvoo, his youth in the Great Salt Lake Valley, and his fifteen-year missionary career beginning in 1849 and concluding in 1864. One chapter will be devoted to his boyhood, and one to each of his five missions for the Church. George Q. Cannon made a statement which, though not intended to refer to himself, certainly seems to apply:

A perusal of the journals of the Elders of this Church who have kept daily record of that which they have endured and witnessed, and the various incidents of their missions would be as interesting as the acts of the Apostles in the New Testament; for God has manifested Himself in the most extraordinary manner in their be-half.[18]

A look into the journals and records written by and about President Cannon is both interesting and inspiring, and does witness that the Lord's manifestations in his behalf were indeed extraordinary.

CHAPTER 2

The Preparation

Conversion of the Cannon Family

THE CANNON FAMILY'S CONVERSION into the Church began in Canada. Parley P. Pratt took the message of the Restoration to John Taylor, George Q. Cannon's uncle, who later took the gospel to George Q. Cannon's family in England. The first link in this inspiring chain of events occurred on a spring evening of 1836 in Kirtland, Ohio. Parley P. Pratt, one of the first Apostles appointed in the latter-day Church, retired to his bed troubled in spirit. Many of his fellow Apostles were

John Taylor Printing Office in Nauvoo

preparing to leave on missions, and he yearned to do likewise. But because he was deeply in debt, there seemed to be no way he could go. While he was pondering over his "future course," a knock came at the door.

The caller was another of the twelve Apostles, Heber C. Kimball, who, "being filled with the spirit of prophecy," desired to bless Brother Pratt. In this blessing Elder Kimball revealed to Parley P. Pratt the Lord's will concerning his missionary desires. He assured him that his financial needs would be taken care of so that he could go "to upper Canada, even to the city of Toronto, the capital." He further prophesied of the far-reaching effects of the mission on which Brother Pratt was called to embark:

> Thou shalt find a people prepared for the fulness of the gospel, and they shall receive thee, and thou shalt organize the Church among them, and it shall spread thence to the regions round about, and many shall be brought to the knowledge of the truth and shall be filled with joy; and from the things growing out of this mission, shall the fulness of the gospel spread into England, and cause a great work to be done in that land.[1]

In fulfillment of this prophecy, Elder Pratt found himself only a few weeks later in Toronto at the home of John Taylor, a member of the local Methodist congregation to whom he had been miraculously guided. Mr. Taylor was truly a person "prepared for the fulness of the gospel," for as a lad of seventeen in England he had received among many other spiritual promptings "a strong impression . . . that I have to go to America to preach the gospel."[2] While crossing the Atlantic en route for Canada, the ship on which he had taken passage was beset by such a violent storm that everyone aboard, even the captain, "expected hourly that she would go down." Young Taylor again heard the

Spirit whisper within him, "You must yet go to America and preach the gospel." His faith in this prompting pacified him: "So confident was I of my destiny . . . that I went on deck at midnight, and amidst the raging elements felt as calm as though I was sitting in a parlor at home. I believed I should reach America and perform my work."[3]

Leonora Cannon Taylor, John's wife, was also no stranger to the guidance of the Lord. As a young girl she too had been inspired to migrate from England to the New World; she had a prophetic dream that prompted her to accept an invitation to go to Canada with a dear friend whose father, Mr. Mason, had recently been chosen as private secretary to the Governor General of that country.[4] Soon after her arrival in Canada, Leonora became affiliated with the local Methodist congregation, where she met the brilliant young Englishman, John Taylor, who soon fell in love with her and asked her to be his wife. At first she refused him, but inspired by another dream where she saw herself happily married to him, she accepted his renewed proposal. They were married January 28, 1833.

John and Leonora were both in a study group whose members were looking for additional truth. He felt that the Methodist church did not possess the fulness of the gospel of Christ. Other members of the congregation shared his sentiments concerning the inadequacy of Protestant doctrine and would often meet with the Taylors to search the scriptures for further light. When John Taylor referred to the prophecy concerning his destiny to preach the gospel in America, Leonora would ask, "Are you not now preaching the gospel in America?" To this her husband would insist: "This is not the work; it is something of more importance."[5] When Parley P. Pratt arrived in Toronto and made his acquaintance with John Taylor, he taught the restored gospel to this group, and nearly all of them were baptized on May 4, 1836, fulfilling Elder Kimball's prophecy about a "people prepared."[6]

Brother Taylor's boyhood revelation was fulfilled soon after his baptism when he was ordained an elder in The Church of Jesus Christ of Latter-day Saints and began preaching in America what he had come to believe was the true gospel of Christ. In 1838, only two years after his baptism, John Taylor was called by revelation to be a member of the Quorum of the Twelve Apostles and to preach the gospel in all the world.[7] Two years later Elder Taylor sailed for his native land of England to carry the gospel to his former countrymen, thus fulfilling the other part of Heber C. Kimball's prophecy to Parley P. Pratt that "from the things growing out of this mission, shall the fullness of the gospel be spread into England."[8]

On the same day as his boat docked in Liverpool—January 11, 1840—Elder Taylor, with Wilford Woodruff, another member of the Twelve, called at the home of his wife's brother, George Cannon. Not finding Mr. Cannon at home, Elder Taylor made an appointment to return that evening. As he walked away, Mrs. Cannon told her thirteen-year-old son: "George, there goes a man of God. He is come to bring salvation to your father's house."[9] As the evening approached, young George felt the excitement of the "approach of destiny," for he believed the words of his mother.[10] Little did he realize that he would one day serve as First Counselor to both his Uncle John Taylor and to Wilford Woodruff in the First Presidency of The Church of Jesus Christ of Latter-day Saints.

George Q. Cannon was the son of George and Ann Quayle Cannon, who were both natives of Peel, Isle of Man, and who were described as having "a wealth of uprightness, honesty, integrity, probity and Christian devotion which made them respected and esteemed in the community where they dwelt."[11] George and Ann were second cousins, their mothers both being Callisters, and were married about 1825. After their marriage they moved to Liverpool, where George Cannon became a carpenter and cabinetmaker. Proud of the Cannon name and eager to carry it on in his own posterity, Mr. Cannon was elated when, on January 11, 1827, Ann gave birth to a healthy son, to whom the father promptly gave his own name. Six other children followed at intervals, making in all two daughters and five sons. One unnamed son died soon after birth, and another, John Quayle, died at age three-and-a-half. Mr. Cannon expressed his inherent faith in life after death in a letter to his sister Leonora Taylor at the time of little John's passing: "Such a boy," exclaimed the stricken father. . . . "My heart was softened with the death of this child, but I shall see him yet."[12]

Ann Cannon also possessed a natural religious faith, but neither she nor her husband could be satisfied with any of the denominations "which they saw warring against each other"[13] in Liverpool, England. Before leaving for America, Leonora had entreated her brother George to join her as a Methodist, but he refused, "on the ground that it could not satisfy his spiritual needs. He was searching for truth, and truth alone."[14] Sister Taylor felt certain that this restored gospel message, carried to England by her husband, would satisfy her brother's quest for truth. She wrote a letter to her brother, introducing her husband.

Elder Taylor returned to his brother-in-law's home that evening, explained the Book of Mormon to the family, presented them with a copy of it, and also thrilled them by singing some inspiring "songs of Zion."[15] Ann Cannon immediately recognized that her brother-in-law spoke the truth. Her husband,

George, however, while not antagonistic, was not so certain; but he determined to study the Book of Mormon thoroughly before making his judgment. As he began reading, "his interest grew with every page, until the spirit of the book had soon taken such complete possession of him that he could scarcely lay it down. He read it far into the night, at mealtimes, and even had it propped open on his joiner's bench where he could glimpse a few sentences as he worked."[16]

When he finished the book, which he had read cover-to-cover twice within three weeks, he pronounced this verdict: "No wicked man could write such a book as this; and no good man would write it, unless it were true and he were commanded of God to do so."[17] On February 11, 1840, just one month after their introduction to the gospel, George and Ann Cannon became members of The Church of Jesus Christ of Latter-day Saints.

Soon after the Cannons were baptized, Elder Taylor wrote the good news to his anxious wife, who was then in Montrose, Iowa; she answered his letter on April 14: "My dear husband: I went over the river yesterday, and I got a letter from you, dated 15th February. I never received a letter that gave me so much real comfort as it has done. I do rejoice and praise God for what He has done in bringing my dear brother George, and sister Ann, into the Church—the only Church with which the Lord is well pleased. I do hope that the rest of our dear scattered ones may yet be gathered into the fold, and yet live and reign with our blessed Lord and Savior."[18]

Another letter that must have brought Sister Taylor great joy was a message of gratitude from her brother George, who wrote:

I bless the Lord that I ever saw your husband's face, and I now see plainly that our dear mother's prayer has not only been answered for you, but has extended to me and my family through you. . . . I see the hand of the Lord so visible in all that has happened to me that I cannot help telling you of it. . . . I was happy in an affectionate wife, promising children, good health, plenty of work, and always a pound to spare—but still there was a want of something which made me feel very low-spirited at times, . . . but when Brother Taylor came to Liverpool, and I was sincerely desirous to lead a new life, he had the words whereby I might be saved; and though slow of belief at first, and not seeing the necessity of baptism, yet God in His infinite mercy opened my eyes.[19]

No one suggested that the two older children, George and Mary Alice, follow their parents in this ordinance, and though both of them had a deep yearning for this privilege they thought it would be too presumptuous to ask. Young George discussed this desire with Mary Alice, who was eleven at the time, and they both prayed earnestly for this blessing.

On the sixth of April that year, five more Apostles arrived in Liverpool, including Parley P. Pratt, who recorded, "We soon found Brother Taylor, who had raised the standard of truth in Liverpool, and had already baptized about thirty."[20] One morning, when Elder Pratt and Elder Taylor were eating breakfast with the Cannon family, Elder Pratt, "as if moved by a sudden inspiration, inquired: 'Elder Taylor, have you preached the gospel to these children? Some of them want to be baptized now, don't you?'"[21] Both George and Mary Alice voted their eagerness.

But yet another member of the family wished to be baptised—little Ann, who was just eight years old. She too had been listening to the missionaries' message and recorded in her journal: "We had many people come to our house to talk about [the gospel]. I was sent to bed with my brother David, the baby, but I would get up when he was asleep and sit on the stairs and listen to them converse on the gospel. My father found me asleep, and said I must be allowed to sit up or I would fall and break my neck."[22] Her parents thought her too young to make such serious covenants, but she "wept so bitterly at being left out that she was allowed to join them, and the three were baptized into The Church of Jesus Christ of Latter-day Saints."[23] The baptism took place on 18 June 1840.

Like his mother, young George believed the gospel as soon as he heard it. In later life he explained the origin of his testimony: "Did you ask how I got my testimony of the truth of Mormonism? Why, I never got one. . . . The reason why I received none was because I did not have to get one. It was born with me. Since I first heard the Gospel or Mormonism as it is called, I have always known it to be true. It seemed part of my very nature."[24]

Something in George's childhood, which happened long before the missionaries ever came, shows that he truly was, as he said, born with a nature to seek after spiritual things: "As a child, I wept because I did not live on the earth when Jesus wandered among men. And I asked myself why it is that men cannot receive those blessings as they who were the associates of Jesus received them? I asked my teachers, and I asked my parents, "Are there men now who receive these blessings?" and they answered me that there were none, and I wondered why it was so."[25]

One of the Savior's blessings that George longed to have was some kind of spiritual gift. He recalled: "I can remember in my early boyhood that I felt very bad because I had no especial gift, and I used to think I was not a favored child of God, else I would have received the gift of tongues or some other such gift."[26] When his uncle brought the family the gospel, he no longer wondered where the men who had these powers were to be found. Because Elder Taylor used the Cannon home as his headquarters in

Liverpool, young George had the privilege of meeting most of
the Twelve Apostles and many other elders of the Church. This
association kindled in him a desire to become an elder himself.
He recalled expressing this desire to his schoolmates:

> When I was a little boy about twelve years of age, I was asked in
> school what I would like to be. The boys were talking about their
> future occupations—they knew I was a Mormon and I remarked
> that I wanted to be an elder in The Church of Jesus Christ of
> Latter-day Saints. That was my highest ambition; that was my
> strongest desire; it was that I might preach this Gospel, that I
> would like to spend my days in preaching the Gospel. I was very
> young, but I did love the Gospel; I loved the truth, and I sought
> to obtain a knowledge concerning it, and the Lord granted that
> request to me, and when He granted it to me, I was perfectly
> happy.[27]

Immigrating to Nauvoo

Like most who accepted the gospel in those days, almost immediately after their baptism the Cannons experienced an over-
whelming desire to unite themselves with the main body of the
Saints in Nauvoo. This desire was apparently spontaneous, since
the unsettled conditions in Illinois prevented the elders from
preaching the principle of gathering to Zion at that time. In a
letter from Father Cannon to his sister Leonora, he declared, "If
it is the Lord's will, I am ready to go any time."[28] Once the family decided to emigrate they began saving their money. Sister
Cannon, by nature very frugal, began putting into a secret account all the surplus money she could save by cutting household
expenses. George Q., the only other member of the family who
knew the account existed, faithfully carried the money to the

bank for her. Sister Cannon took great delight in contemplating the surprise she would have for her husband when she would tell him how much money she had saved.

One day when young George was about to receive a well-deserved whipping, he threatened to expose her secret: "If you whip me, I'll tell Father about the savings account, and tell him how much there is of it!"[29] Desiring to guard her secret, she let the little blackmailer go unpunished. This lever served him so well that he tried it again but with less success—he received the thrashing anyway.[30]

Young George Q. was, of course, very excited at the prospect of going to Zion, and even asked his parents to let him quit school and take a job to save money. Placing a high value on education, they objected, but he argued that education was more a product of inner desire than of formal schooling. And finally, because George was "a strong-willed boy and possessed of an uncanny ability to persuade, he left school and found work in a shipping office. Here his penmanship, in which he took great pride, was an asset, for all copying was done in longhand. . . . His handwriting came to look like copper plate engraving."[31]

At the end of his formal schooling in England he was presented with a Bible "by the committee of Jordon Street school . . . as a mark of their approbation of his conduct in the school."[32]

Obtaining adequate finances was not the only difficulty the Cannons encountered in preparing to leave England. Brother Cannon's employer, sorry to lose such an exacting and industrious worker, made him an attractive offer, a raise of five shillings a week, in an effort to change his mind about leaving; but Brother Cannon was so staunch in his testimony and in his determination to go to Zion that instead of being dissuaded him-

self he almost convinced his employer to go also: "He acknowl-
edged that my testimony and his own observation had led him to
conclusions which made him tremble. He begged of me to write
him when I got to Nauvoo the truth, and he would place confidence in my account, and he thought he could induce about
forty of his relatives to join him in emigrating to Nauvoo."[33]

Young George's employer also valued the boy's services so
much that when he heard of the family's plan to go to America
he tried to persuade them to allow George to remain behind and
live with his family. He "promised to make him an expert and
master of the newly born and stupendous problems of transportation."[34]

Another difficulty arose from strong-minded relatives and
friends who felt that such a move was unprecedented foolishness.
They pleaded with the Cannons to stay, warning them that they
would be sorry for "leaving England and a constant employ";
they would not help them in any way with their departure, refus-
ing even to buy a few items of furniture that needed disposition.[35] "Poor George," commented one of these so-called friends,
"he made a great mistake when he emigrated, leaving a comfortable home, good employment and loving friends to go out among
the wild red Indians—too bad, yes, it was really too bad."[36]

Another obstacle Brother Cannon and the two older children
confronted in making the voyage to America was their knowledge of Sister Cannon's strong premonition that she would not
live to see Zion. She would not hear of putting off the voyage
for this reason, even though she was expecting her eighth child,
for "she was impressed that if this season should pass and the
family still be in England, she would not be alive to urge their
journey another year."[37] This nagging fear was further aug-
mented in the father's heart by his own sense that his wife would

die. He wrote: "Many years since I dreamed a dream which time or circumstance has never been able to remove. I was impressed with a conviction that my wife should die while in a state of pregnancy."[38]

Despite these obstacles and forebodings, the family set sail about nine o'clock on Saturday morning 17 September 1842 aboard the ship *Sidney*. No relatives appeared to see them off. Almost from the first hours Sister Cannon was ill, the motion of the boat and her pregnancy having upset her stomach so completely that for ten days she was unable to retain any food at all. Concerning the other members of the family, Brother Cannon recorded in his journal: "Leonora and David have had no sickness and are less trouble than I expected; but George, Mary Alice, Ann and Angus have all been very sick, particularly George and Anny."[39] Though Sister Cannon's condition worsened each day, her husband reported that through it all no complaint ever escaped her lips. His journal for October 28 bore the inevitable news: Sister Cannon "fell asleep without a sigh . . . at half past four o'clock, and was buried in that element which needed no consecration, it never being cursed, . . . at five o'clock in the afternoon the same day." Giving vent to his deep sorrow, the bereft husband further penned:

Although in expectation of bearing many things which are not of a pleasant nature—privation or poverty we agreed to share with the Saints, but we are tried in a more tender part, and were it not for our helpless children's sake I should like to repose under the peaceful blue waters with her who shared my every joy and sorrow. Heavenly Father keep me from repining! But seeing other people enjoying the society of those they love, my heart sickens and I long to be at rest with my dear wife.[40]

And so George Cannon, age fifteen, and his five younger brothers and sisters were left motherless in the middle of the ocean, heading for a strange new home.

About three weeks later the *Sidney* sailed into the port of New Orleans, and with mixed emotions Father Cannon disembarked with his six children, completing their fifty-six-day voyage. Because the season was late and the waters of the Mississippi so low, the steamboat, *Alexander Scott*, on which they took passage up the river, could only carry them as far as St. Louis. They were forced to remain there throughout the winter, taking refuge in an abandoned cabin. Some kindly women in the company of Saints willingly assisted Brother Cannon in caring for his family. "In fact," said he, "they behaved like mothers to my children and the Lord will bless them for it."[41] Scarlet fever swept their company that winter, taking fourteen lives, but fortunately it left the Cannon family alive to continue their journey to Zion. In spite of the miserable conditions they were forced to endure, Father Cannon saw to it that his son George enrolled in school that winter to continue his education for a few months.

Experiences in Nauvoo

When at last spring came, the encamped Saints boarded the Church-owned steamboat *Maid of Iowa* and proceeded to Nauvoo, arriving in April 1843.[42] A large crowd had gathered on the wharf at Nauvoo to welcome the English Saints. The Prophet Joseph Smith was among the throng. Sixteen-year-old George had longed to see this great man since first hearing the marvelous stories about him. He scanned the crowd, trying to catch sight of Joseph, and to his surprise he recognized the Prophet immediately even though he had never seen his picture. In a book on Joseph Smith's life, which he wrote many years later, George Q. Cannon described this inspired recognition:

> It was the Author's privilege to thus meet the Prophet for the first time. . . . Nearly every prominent man in the community was there. Familiar with the names of all and the persons of many of the prominent Elders, the Author sought, with a boy's curiosity and eagerness, to discover those whom he knew, and especially to get sight of the Prophet and his brother Hyrum, neither of whom he had ever met. When his eyes fell upon the Prophet, without a word from anyone to point him out or any reason to separate him from others who stood around, he knew him instantly. He would have known him among ten thousand. There was that about him which to the Author's eyes, distinguished him from all the men he had ever seen.[43]

The excitement of this occasion reached its climax for George when on the shore the president of the Church personally greeted the Cannon family. John and Leonora Taylor had told him of this faithful family, of their generosity to the missionaries in England, and also of Sister Cannon's death at sea, for which loss the Prophet expressed his sympathy. Throughout his entire life young George maintained a great admiration and awe for the Prophet Joseph. Fifty-eight years later in general conference, Brother Cannon said: "I had this feeling when a boy in the days of Joseph. To me Joseph was perfect. I could not see and did not hear anything that ever made any impression upon me to the contrary."[44]

John and Leonora Taylor readily extended their home and hospitality to the Cannons, but very soon Brother Cannon purchased from Chauncey Webb a small home across the street from the Taylor residence. Although fourteen-year-old Mary Alice did all she could to manage her father's household, she was unable to fill the void left by the death of an adored mother and wife. About a year later, on February 24, 1844, Brother Cannon married Mary Edwards White, whom he had met on the *Sidney* while crossing from England.[45]

In the early summer of the same year the Nauvoo Saints bore the awful tragedy of their Prophet Joseph's and his brother Hyrum's assassination at Carthage. George's six-year-old brother, David, was near his father in Nauvoo at the moment the Prophet was killed, and he later told of the instantaneous knowledge Brother Cannon received of the murderous deed: "At the time of the death of the Prophet Joseph Smith, I remember my father standing at the gate at the front of the house, his arms kind of leaning on the gate. He turned, and as he did so, said, 'My God, they have killed our Prophet.' That was the time the Prophet was martyred."[46]

The Cannons faced added horror when they learned that the Prophet's murderers had severely wounded their dear uncle, John Taylor, who had voluntarily accompanied the Prophet to prison. When the bodies of the Prophet and his brother were returned to Nauvoo, Brother Cannon, who had again taken up his joiner's trade, made the coffins and helped prepare the remains for burial. It is also to Brother Cannon that future generations of Mormons are indebted for knowing the exact likeness of Joseph and Hyrum; one of the very few who knew the process of plaster molding, he made from the faces of the martyrs death masks that are still in existence.[47]

A few weeks later young George witnessed the confusion many experienced in regard to who should now assume leadership of the Church. He was present at the meeting held August

8, 1844, in Nauvoo, when Sidney Rigdon, a former counselor to the Prophet, presented his claim to "guardianship" of the Church. On the same occasion George heard Brigham Young, the president of the Twelve, powerfully proclaim the true process of succession to the Presidency of the Church, which the Lord had revealed, and he was one of many who witnessed what has since been called the transfiguration of Brigham Young:

> President Brigham Young . . . arose and addressed the people. It was the first sound of his voice they had heard since he had gone East on a mission, and the effect upon them was most wonderful. If Joseph had risen from the dead and again spoken in their hearing, the effect could not have been more startling than it was to many present at that meeting. It was the voice of Joseph himself, and not only was it the voice of Joseph which was heard; but it seemed in the eyes of the people as though it was the very person of Joseph which stood before them.[48]

George further related how this manifestation affected the Saints:

> The Lord gave his people a testimony that left no room for doubt as to who was the man he had chosen to lead them. They saw and heard with their natural eyes and ears, and then the words which were uttered came, accompanied by the convincing power of God, to their hearts, and they were filled with the spirit and great joy. There had been gloom, and in some hearts, probably, doubt and uncertainty, but now it was plain to all that here was the man upon whom the Lord had bestowed the necessary authority to act in their midst in Joseph's stead.[49]

This experience made such an impression on the seventeen-year-old boy that he never lost the certain knowledge that Brigham

Young was truly chosen of the Lord, and this conviction was the basis of his profound dedication to Brigham Young until President Young's death in 1877—thirty-three years later.

In the aftermath of the Prophet Joseph's martyrdom, Illinois revoked the Nauvoo City Charter, thereby leaving the city unprotected by law. This condition naturally attracted unsavory strangers who hoped to capitalize on this absence of law enforcement. George Q. Cannon tells how the boys his age carried on an effective voluntary defense against possible troublemakers to the Saints:

> It was, and still is, a common practice among Yankees, when engaged in conversation or in making a bargain, to take out their pocket knives and commence whittling; frequently, also, when engaged in thought they indulge in the same practice, accompanying the whittling by whistling. No person could object, therefore, to the practices of whittling and whistling. Many of the boys of the city each had a large bowie knife made, and when a man came to town who was known to be a villain, and there for evil purposes, a few of them would get together, and go where the obnoxious person was, and having previously provided themselves with pine shingles, would commence whittling. The presence of a number of boys, each whittling with a bright, large bowie knife, was not a sight to escape the notice of a stranger, especially when these knives came uncomfortably close to his body. His first movement, of course, would be to step back and ask what this meant. The boys would make no reply, but with grave faces, keep up their whistling. What could the man do? If he was armed, he could shoot, but the resolute expression of the boys' faces, and the gleaming knives would convince him that discretion was the better part of valor. The most we ever knew them to do was to stand for a while and curse and threaten . . . ; then they would

walk off, followed by a troop of boys vigorously whittling and whistling.[50]

Although in telling this story George avoided stating that he was one of these boys, in the above account he slips and says "we." This pronoun and the apparent delight with which he tells the story are pretty conclusive evidence that he participated and enjoyed it.

The loss of the city charter and harassment from outsiders resulted in an uncertain future for Nauvoo, and thus the building trade declined. Unable to find enough work to sustain his family, George's father was forced to go elsewhere for employment. Because St. Louis was the only other place in America where he knew anyone, he naturally gravitated to that city. After an absence from his family of only a few weeks, he suddenly and unexpectedly died—another heartbreaking experience for young George and his brothers and sisters. The cause of his death was mysterious; he supposedly died of sunstroke, but no one knew for certain. Even the site of the grave is unknown.[51] A few months after his untimely death, his wife of half a year gave birth to her first child and his last, a daughter, Elizabeth. The six orphaned children now had to find new homes. The three youngest were taken into the home of their oldest sister, Mary Alice, and her husband Charles Lambert, who moved up their marriage date to provide a home for little Angus, David, and Leonora. Mary Alice was only fifteen years old. George and Ann were taken into the home of their Uncle John Taylor, whom they affectionately called "Uncle Taylor."[52]

At this time John Taylor published two newspapers for the Church, the *Times and Seasons* and the *Nauvoo Neighbor.* He now took young George into his office as his apprentice and introduced him to the printing and publishing trade, which business George Q. Cannon pursued both privately and for the Church until the end of his life. Because of his fine penmanship, his uncle also employed him as his accountant and confidential secretary, in which capacity he penned some of John Taylor's personal journal.[53] Through this intimate association, Uncle Taylor grew to love George like a son and developed a confidence in him that he manifested in later years by choosing his nephew as his First Counselor when he (John Taylor) became President of the Church. Living with his uncle and working at the side of this noble man taught George many things and doubtless contributed to his own future greatness. The desire George expressed as a little boy to become an elder in the Church and carry the gospel to others grew in this environment:

> When a youth, it was my good fortune to live in the family of President John Taylor. It was my chief delight in those days to listen to him and other Elders relate their experiences as missionaries. Such conversations were very fascinating to me. They made a deep impression upon me. The days of which they spoke were the days of poverty, when Elders traveled without purse or scrip, among strange people who were ignorant of our principles, and too many of whom were ready to mob and persecute. They traveled by faith and were pioneers for the Lord in strange lands, and He was their only reliance. Their missions were rich in instances of His power exhibited in their behalf. What I heard strengthened my faith and increased the desire in my heart to be a missionary. No calling was so noble in my eyes as that of a standard-bearer of the Gospel.[54]

But living in the home of an Apostle did not rid George of all opposition. One of the men he worked with setting type often boasted of his riotous and immoral conduct, continually trying to entice George to reject the gospel. "When you get as old as I am, George, you will see how false it is and will give it up," he said. To this harassment, George retorted, "Damn you, Tom Rolfe. You tell me that when I grow up, I will lose my faith in this Church. I certainly will if I do the wicked things you're boasting about."[55] George seemed to understand clearly the relationship between righteousness and having the Spirit of the Lord.

On February 9, 1845, at age eighteen, part of George's boyhood dream came true: he was ordained an elder in the Melchizedek Priesthood under the hands of his uncle. The very same day he was also ordained a seventy and called to serve as the clerk of the newly formed Nineteenth Quorum of Seventies.[56] Although George Q. Cannon was destined to become one of the great orators of the Church and of the United States Congress, at the time he assumed this first priesthood responsibility he was an extremely inept speaker, fearful of addressing an audience. This fact adds significance to the promise he made at that time: "There was one resolve that [I] made in the beginning, which [I] have always kept, that whenever called upon, [I] would, with the help of the Lord, always ask a blessing, or pray, or speak, and not try to excuse [myself]."[57]

Before the death of Joseph Smith the Church leaders had been making plans to remove the Saints to the seclusion of the Rocky Mountains. As persecution intensified, they hastened preparations for this exodus. On 16 February 1846 George assisted his uncle in moving his family and a few possessions across the ice-covered Mississippi River to the Iowa shore.[58] In leaving the relative security of Nauvoo, George also left behind his childhood. His mother and father were both dead; his brothers and sisters dispersed; his home with the Taylors uprooted. He now faced the frontier of Western America as a man, the central figure of his own story and the guardian of his destiny.

CHAPTER 3

The Gold Mission

The Journey West

THE MORMONS PLANNED the evacuation of Nauvoo to begin in the spring of 1846, but rumors that their enemies might interfere with this exodus hastened their departure to the beginning of February. Because so many of the Saints were not prepared to travel very far, and because, soon after they crossed the river, a thaw set in, making all the available roads too muddy to navigate, they made their first camp at Sugar Creek, Iowa, within sight of their deserted city. By climbing a nearby hill, one

Gold mining in California, ca. 1849

of the Saints had a perfect view of "Nauvoo, the Beautiful," and
wrote:

> The silvery notes of the temple bell
> That we loved so deep and well:
> And a pang of grief would swell the heart
> And the scalding tears in anguish start
> As we silently gazed on our dear old homes.[1]

The suffering and destitution of the Saints greatly touched
George Q. Cannon. He described the miserable conditions they
endured both at Sugar Creek and during their journey across the
Territory of Iowa, where they encamped at Council Bluffs, Iowa,
on the east bank of the Missouri River and at Winter Quarters
on the west bank: "They were imperfectly clothed, the wagons
were only partly covered, and many had no tents, food also in
some instances was scarce. The cold had been so severe while
they were encamped at Sugar Creek that the Mississippi river
was frozen over; they were also exposed to fierce winds and to
snow; and afterwards, when the winter broke, they were often
drenched to the skin with rain, which . . . soaked the ground so
thoroughly that it made traveling very laborious . . . and frequently tents had to be pitched in the mud as there was no dry
spot to be found."[2]

June 17, 1846, the company with which George was traveling reached Council Bluffs. Here they planted crops and prepared a "winter quarters." It was from this point that the Saints
would embark on the one-thousand-mile trek to their Zion in
the mountains.

Two weeks after their arrival, Captain J. Allen of the United
States Army arrived to counsel with Brigham Young about the

possibility of the Mormons furnishing five hundred young men to march to Santa Fe and California as soldiers in the war against Mexico. Because of the lack of government protection extended to them during their persecutions in Missouri and Illinois, the general membership of the Church was not enthusiastic about this proposal. But the Church leaders did not allow bitterness to outweigh their loyalty to their country. In only about twenty days, five hundred young Latter-day Saint men were organized and placed under the command of Captain Allen, now "Lieutenant-Colonel Allen"—a promotion promised to him if he succeeded in persuading the Mormons to furnish the prescribed army.[3]

Nineteen-year-old George Q. was enlisted in this battalion, and doubtless would have made the trek with them had it not been for John Taylor's sudden mission call to England. This pressing call came as a result of a revelation to Brigham Young that "the presidency [over Church affairs] in England was in transgression, and that it was necessary that some of the Twelve should proceed immediately to England."[4] In their father's absence, the Taylor family urgently needed George to take the lead as the man of their family, the oldest sons being only twelve and eight years old. George therefore stayed behind to help his uncle's family.

During the year that John Taylor was gone to England, George was busy planting crops and building shelters for the thousands of Saints who were or soon would be at Council Bluffs. In preparation for the Taylor family's move westward, he began breaking and training steers to pull their wagons. During this time George met Colonel Thomas L. Kane, who became a nationally prominent champion of the Mormon cause and subsequently a lifelong friend of George Q. Cannon. Colonel Kane, in his history, left this interesting description of the settlements at Council Bluffs and Winter Quarters:

> They were collected a little distance above the Pottawatamie
> Agency. The hills of the high prairie crowding in upon the river at
> this point and overhanging it, appear of an unusual and com-
> manding elevation. They are called the "Council Bluffs.". . .
> Across the river from this spot the hills recur again, but are
> skirted at their base by as much low ground as suffices for a land-
> ing. This landing, and the large flat or bottom on the east side of
> the river, were covered with covered carts and wagons; and each
> one of the Council Bluff hills opposite was crowded with its own
> great camp, gay with bright white canvas, and alive with the busy
> stir of swarming occupants. In the clear blue morning air the
> smoke streamed up from more than a thousand cooking fires.
> Countless roads and bypaths checkered all manner of geometric
> figures on the hill-sides. Herd boys were dozing upon the slopes;
> sheep and horses, cows and oxen were feeding round them, and
> other herds in the luxuriant meadows of the then swollen river.
> From a single point I counted four thousand head of cattle in
> view at one time. As I approached, it seemed to me the children
> were to prove still more numerous.[5]

In April of 1847 Elder Taylor returned from his 17,000-
mile mission to England bringing with him some surveying and
scientific instruments he had purchased to help build their new
home in the mountains.[6] Since he had arrived too late to go west
with Brigham Young and the pioneer company, he and Elder Parley P. Pratt became the leaders of the first large company to go
to the Valley. The company of 1,553 Saints and nearly 4,000
head of stock left Winter Quarters on June 21, 1847.

Because of the mammoth responsibility of presiding over
such a huge migration, the care of John Taylor's family still
rested heavily on his nephew George. Most of the way across the

plains and mountains George drove a team of a young steer and a heifer that he had trained and dubbed Jack and Jill. Jack, more unsettled than Jill, ran wild on one occasion and tipped over the wagon. This mishap so exasperated his young trainer that he "indulged in the only swearing [outside of his talk with Tom Rolfe, see chapter 2, page 26] that he could ever remember using. Losing his temper completely at the sight of the disaster, he blurted out, 'Blast your eyes, Jack.'"[7]

Apparently this was not the only accident George had with his team. When they drew near the Platte River he somehow ran into the wagon of Elder Charles Rich, breaking the Apostle's axle tree—a great calamity in the timberless country through which they were traveling. Brother Rich scolded him severely; George said he bore the reproof "patiently without any attempt at justification."[8] Later that day General Rich sent an apology to the young driver, considering that, after all, it had been an accident. This was the first time George had encountered Brother Rich, a man who became his lifelong friend, one he greatly admired from this time on. He later said of Elder Rich, "Though I was but a boy, he was too much of a gentleman to give me what he considered an undeserved reproof without making an apology."[9]

On September 7, with a whole month of travel still ahead, the company was startled and dismayed to wake up and find snow falling. The unwelcome prospect of traveling through high mountain passes in this inclement weather caused fear and trembling among many of the company. But Brother Taylor, with a mask of confidence, "laughingly proposed to insure the lives of the whole company at five dollars per head."[10] That same day they met President Brigham Young and some of the vanguard group who had reached the Great Salt Lake Valley, where their new city was to be built, and were now returning to Winter

Quarters to help organize the Saints for the westward migration. From them the westbound company received much needed encouragement and instruction regarding the remainder of the journey.

To celebrate this joyful reunion, the sisters in the company brought out their fine linen and china from boxes that had not been opened since their hurried departure from Nauvoo, and on makeshift tables in the wilderness spread a feast for these brethren that was unparalleled by any other meal of their journey.[11] Following this unusual banquet the entire company celebrated with songs, recitations, and dancing.

Because so many men had gone with the Mormon Battalion, George was among the relatively few "eligible young men" of the company and very likely danced with a good many young ladies on occasions such as these. One young lady, Mary Jane Dilworth, appears to have had a strong admiration for George, and she later recalled: "I always knew George Q. Cannon would become a great man. I never saw him waste a minute. As soon as his oxen were unyoked and the necessary work done, he could always be found sitting on the tongue of his wagon reading a book."[12] Mary Jane noticed and appreciated a person who sought to improve himself by study; she herself became the first schoolteacher in Utah. But it seems that George already had a special interest in the twelve-year-old daughter of Brother Abraham Hoagland. This girl reported in later life that George would often help her with her tasks along the way, and "a firm friendship was soon developed. She recalled with pleasure the songs and dances around the campfire at night, the games they played, the joy and laughter rather than the hardships."[13] In 1854 this childhood sweetheart named Elizabeth became his wife.

Life in the Valley of the Great Salt Lake

Near the end of September the company caught their first glimpse of the Great Salt Lake Valley. Whatever feelings—joys, expectations, disappointments, fears—George may have had were soon superseded by the urgent work of preparing homes for the oncoming winter. He wrote this description of a mistake in the building design of the fort they built for shelter:

> The houses were built close together, with the highest wall on the outside, which formed the wall of the Fort; the roofs sloped towards the inside, and all the doors and windows were on the inside, so as to make the houses more secure against attack in case any were made. Not having had any experience in this climate, and supposing from the appearance of the ground in the summer and fall and from all that could be learned concerning it that it was very dry, the roofs of the houses were made rather flat. The result was that nearly every house leaked during the first winter, and umbrellas, where such a luxury as an umbrella was owned, were frequently in demand to shelter those engaged in cooking, and even in bed persons would be seen sitting or lying under an umbrella.[14]

Fortunately the winter of 1847–48 was very mild; there was little sickness, and very few died. There was, however, a scarcity of food. Brother Cannon recalled, "There was nothing that could contribute to sustain life that was willfully suffered to go to waste." Even mired oxen that were too weak to live were pulled out of the mud and butchered. In the early spring, big grey wolves from the mountains killed some cattle, and the parts of the carcasses that the wolves had not devoured were salvaged for food. A few Saints literally "ate crow" in order to obtain "what nourishment they could extract from it." One popular food was thistle tops. Although their nutritional value was limited, they filled the stomach. George wrote, "to have the stomach full was an agreeable sensation, even if the contents were only thistle tops."[15]

The rough traveling across the plains had taken such a severe toll on the shoes and clothing of the Saints that in the valley they had to rely on animal skins for moccasins and other pieces of clothing. Concerning his own wardrobe, George wrote: "The writer recollects how proud he was when he succeeded in obtaining an elk skin, out of which, after smoking it, he had a pair of pantaloons made. He has had the good fortune to wear some of the best fabrics of this and other countries since then; but he never had owned an article of dress which gave him so much satisfaction and for which he was more thankful than those elk-skin trousers."[16]

George continued to work closely with his Uncle Taylor, who established the first sawmill in the valley. He also made adobe bricks to be used in the house of Mary Alice and Charles Lambert when they reached the valley. George continued to live with the Taylors, but received an "inheritance," a city lot, when they were assigned to the early settlers of the valley. Before he had an opportunity to build on it he was called to leave the valley on several missions. When he returned he found the Fourteenth Ward chapel built on his site. He was never remunerated for this involuntary donation.[17]

In the spring, the inhabitants of the valley planted many acres of crops, which thrived—until the latter part of June, when droves of crickets converged on the tender wheat and corn. Brother Cannon told the story of battling these crickets:

Crickets

Men, women, and children turned out to fight them, but with all the help and energy they could muster, it seemed as if all their

labors would be in vain. Yet the people persevered and were generally cheerful. . . . Think of their condition! The food they brought
with them almost exhausted, their grain and other seeds all
planted, they themselves twelve hundred miles from a settlement
or place where they could get food on the east, and eight hundred
miles from California, and the crickets eating up every green thing
and every day destroying their sole means of subsistence for the
months and winter ahead! Who but the people of God would not
have quailed and murmured, and probably fled at such a prospect?
Yet if they had fear or doubts, or repining it was but little known.
The people were hopeful, and relied upon God to aid and deliver
them; and they were not disappointed. At the time when
prospects began to appear most gloomy, and all human power
seemed useless, the sea gulls came in flocks, visited the fields,
pounced upon the crickets, and devoured them. . . . On Sunday
the fields were deserted by the people who devoted the day to
worship. This was a feast day for the gulls—they devoured without let or hindrance. On Monday morning, on visiting the fields,
the people found on the edges of the water ditches, pile after pile
of dead crickets which had been eaten by the gulls, and then vom-
ited when they were full. . . . This story is another instance of the
simple means which God frequently uses to bring to pass His
great purposes. In the visit of these gulls the Saints saw the hand
of God; to them it was as apparent as the feeding of Elijah by the
ravens.[18]

Not only were the Saints living in the valley saved by this
miracle, but the emigrating Saints were as well. Those traveling
across the plains that summer were to be nourished throughout
the winter on these crops. So thankful were the pioneers that
famine had been averted that they did not wait until Thanksgiv-
ing to hold a harvest festival. On August 10, 1848, they gathered

in the bowery of the fort. They opened with prayer and had dancing; they raised in unison shouts of "Hosannah to God and the Lamb"; and they even fired a cannon, showing plainly that "they were happy and thankful in the new circumstances in which they were placed."[19]

Two months later, at October conference, Heber C. Kimball ended his address with an unbelievable prophecy. He said that soon material goods, wagons, clothing, utensils and supplies would be so plentiful that they would be purchased in the Salt Lake Valley for little or nothing. Many people feared that this time the miracle promised was too great. After the spirit of prophecy left him, President Kimball himself was astonished at what he had said.[20] But sure enough gold was discovered in California at Sutter's Mill.[21] The cry of "Gold!" spread over the country; early in 1849, fortune seekers poured through the Great Salt Lake Valley on the way to California.

Many of these travelers believed they could make great profits by taking various kinds of merchandise to California, where they assumed it would be in great demand. Scores of wagons were heavily loaded with a large variety of articles and supplies, but the journey west proved to be more difficult than the gold seekers had anticipated. Their heavy loads weakened the animals and slowed progress. In Salt Lake City they heard reports of ships sailing into San Francisco Bay loaded with an abundance of the same supplies as the travelers were attempting to transport. Many hard miles still lay between these anxious speculators and their destination. These factors, combined with the enthusiasm they experienced when they saw gold dust from California being used for tender in Salt Lake City, caused a literal fulfillment of President Kimball's prophecy: "States goods would be sold in the streets of Salt Lake City cheaper than in New York, and . . . the people could be abundantly supplied with food and clothing."²² These gold-thirsty travelers practically threw away their earthly possessions to lighten their loads, and the Saints were able to buy much needed merchandise at rock bottom prices.

With the gold rush traffic steadily streaming through Great Salt Lake City, there was naturally a great temptation for Mormons to join them and share in the riches of the far West. But President Young's counsel strongly opposed yielding to such enticements:

> That there is plenty of gold in western California is beyond doubt, but the valley of the Sacramento is an unhealthy place, and the saints can be better employed in raising grain and building houses in this vicinity, than in digging gold in Sacramento, unless they are counseled so to do.
>
> The true use of gold is for paving streets, covering houses and making culinary dishes; and when the saints shall have preached the gospel, raised grain, and built up cities enough, the Lord will open up the way for a supply of gold to the perfect satisfaction of his people; until then, let them not be overanxious for the treasures of the earth are in the Lord's storehouse, and he will open the doors thereof when and where he pleases.²³

Though some Latter-day Saints went contrary to this counsel by heeding the call of easy riches and following these settlers to the goldfields of California, in general the Saints were content to remain in the Zion they had dreamed of, where another kind of fortune reigned. But at length, in the late summer of 1849, President Brigham Young, deciding that the kingdom of God could well be advanced by having some additional financial means, called a group of missionaries—not to preach the gospel, but to cross the deserts to dig gold for the building up of Zion. George Q. Cannon, unmarried, able-bodied, and faithful to the leaders of the Church, was a prime candidate for such a mission. Upon receiving this kind of mission call, he felt a little let down. True, he had hoped to serve a mission, but he wanted to fulfill his boyhood dream of preaching the gospel, not digging gold. And to spend a year away from Elizabeth for that purpose seemed a sacrifice. She felt much the same way. He tried to comfort her by saying: "I am only called for a year to California. Would you prefer that I went for perhaps three years to France?" She answered, "I would rather you went to save souls than to find gold, even though the time be longer."[24]

The Journey to the Goldfields of California

Early in October 1849, George Q. Cannon and nineteen other "gold-digging missionaries" started for California. George was still not enthusiastic about going: "There was no place that I would not rather have gone to at that time than California. . . . There is no honorable occupation that I would not rather follow than hunting and digging gold."[25] However, his devotion to the building up of Zion impelled him to subjugate his personal desires to the instructions of the Church leaders.

John Taylor had secured for George what he thought were two good animals, a young buckskin mare to ride and a grey horse with deformed ears, which George called "Croppy," to carry his pack. The small company traveled south to Provo, where another company of gold seekers, about twenty men, not members of the Church, joined them. A certain Captain Smith led these men, and of him and his men George wrote in his journal: "Capt. Smith's company started with us this morning; they had travelled with us since we left Utah; good feeling exists between the two companies; there are many gentlemanly men in the company. Capt. Smith has taken a very good part and is as far as I know and have seen a perfect gentleman."[26]

It seems to have been very important to George what kind of men were with them, since somewhat later in the journey he mentioned that rowdy and untoward members of the company made traveling extremely unpleasant for the missionaries. George's mind sought lofty thoughts and conversation even on a pack trip: "I had a conversation this evening until a late hour with Brother HY [Henry W.] Bigler upon philosophy and the planetary system until we lost ourselves. I could not help thinking while viewing the heavens how insignificant a creature man is in the midst of the creations he sees around him; peopled no doubt with spirits equal in intelligence to himself and yet how important and of what consequence he thinks himself; reflections like these make me feel my nothingness and sense the vast amount of knowledge I have to learn in regard to God and his works."[27]

Eleven days out of Provo, the gold seekers came upon a marker bearing the notation that the distance from Great Salt Lake City was 208 miles. Elder Charles C. Rich had left this marker for them as he traveled that way only a few days before with a large company of people, mostly not members of the Church, who had hired Brother Jefferson Hunt at $10.00 per wagon to lead them to the goldfields of California. They were planning to travel south along the Spanish Trail, the same route proposed for the Mormon packers. Brother Rich had been called by the Church to proceed to California on a mission and was in company with this large group.

Near Beaver Creek the pack train caught up with the wagons

and made an interesting change in plans. Captain Smith had a map drawn by a Mr. E. William Barney that showed a shortcut route to the goldfields. The route ran straight west instead of southward, as did the Spanish Trail; the distance to California was a great deal shorter, although passage was difficult and the locations of water and navigable passes were very sparse and had to be hit upon exactly. No one there had ever traveled the route, but Captain Smith felt that with the aid of this crude map he could pilot the company safely through.

Jefferson Hunt was unwilling to attempt taking his wagon train through, but the twenty young missionaries decided to follow the Smith Company on this venture, thereby hoping to save time, which was extremely valuable because they wished to reach the gold mines before the rainy season set in and earn enough money to subsist during the rainy months when no digging could be done.[28]

On hearing the decision of the young Mormon men, Elder Rich felt inspired that he should leave the safety of the wagon train and join the missionaries, and that if he did not accompany them some or all of them would perish. He outfitted himself with a horse and a pack mule and departed from the Jefferson Hunt company, following Captain Smith, his twenty men, and the twenty young Mormons across the mountains and the desert for California. Traveling with the non-Mormons, George noticed that they did not understand the principle of authority that he had always taken for granted in traveling with the Saints. He said that unlike the cooperative Mormons, these "gentiles" would often complain and were not always obedient to their leaders. Noticing this spirit among the men, General Rich decided to unify the Latter-day Saint men under his care. He called them together:

This evening had a meeting of the company to know their new route and whether they were to be governed by all of the men or by half or by one; he [General Rich] had found out already that there were different opinions and he wanted that there should be no room for ill feelings hereafter. The feelings of the brethren were that we should go the cut off and that we would be controlled by him in all things. I was glad to see the unanimity of feelings existing among us.[29]

Once the companies set out on the cutoff, their troubles really began. They struggled to find ways to cross the mountains they encountered. Soon George's pack horse, Croppy, began to lag behind. He urged him on, but had little success getting him to keep up with the others because he was constantly trying to throw himself into the water. One night, after they had made great efforts to pull him out of the creek, he wandered back to it and George reported in his journal for November 5, 1849: "This morning found 'Croppy' in the creek drownded [sic]."

Their next problem was not being able to find water:

In starting again we struck over some high hills to the westward and traveled in this direction nearly all day. We estimated our day's journey at 32 miles. We camped in a dry bed of a creek, but could find no water. There was much suffering in camp this night, many of Captain Smith's company offered to give anything they had for a drink. Gloomy and despondent feelings prevailed with a great number, as the prospect of finding water without going a great distance was not very promising.[30]

The next day they started out early, though it was an extremely hot day, and did manage to find some water after traveling for miles into a canyon. The day after that, November 11, they traveled all day over "a most fatigued road" and found at nightfall that they were only three miles from where they had been that morning. George described their circumstances in these words: "It seemed that, unless there was a change in our mode of travel we must inevitably perish in the midst of this wilderness. Since we left the regular trail we had been wandering about in these kanyons, mountains and deserts for eleven days. But our progress in the direction of California had been very slow. . . . Our provisions were disappearing, our clothes wearing out, and our animals would soon be too thin to afford much sustenance if we had to kill them."[31]

This night, Brother Rich called his men together. George wrote in his journal:

> Bro. Rich said this evening that he was not going to be led round in this manner any longer. We should all perish in the mountains if there was not an alteration; if he could not have his way he should go back to the wagons as quick as he could. He said if his counsel had been taken we would not have been here. I was glad to hear him speak as he did for I had seen that he had not taken a very active part in matters and that Capt. Smith's opinion had been taken in preference to the General; it had been his mind [General Rich's] to travel on the table land and keep out of the mountains and if we could not go that way we could not go at all.[32]

The young Mormon missionaries were more than eager to follow the Apostle of the Lord, and even the others agreed to try his plan.

Two days later, while they were traveling under General Rich's direction, it started to rain. Young Elder Cannon explained in his journal how thrilled they were to be blessed with this water and what great advantage they took of it:

> We started again after stopping about an hour. It still continued
> raining; as we went along every rock that had a hollow with water
> standing in it was greedily drank by the men; it soon began to
> stand in puddles on the ground and we soon got satisfied as well
> as the animals. When it first commenced I turned the rim of my
> hat and caught enough in it to afford me occasionally a drink. We
> camped in a hollow and cooked our supper with rain water and
> filled every thing that would hold water for the morrow. Never in
> my life did I see the hand of the Lord more plainly shown than in
> the present instance (Capt. Smith said to Gen. Rich that the fin-
> ger of the Lord was in this) for we must have suffered, had it not
> been for this, very much and probably have perished for to all ap-
> pearances there was no water any nearer than Providence creek.
> Ceased raining in evening.[33]

General Rich led them for about a day and a half before they
found water again. At this watering spot Brother Rich made an
inspired decision, one which no doubt saved the lives of these
young Latter-day Saints. He concluded that under the circumstances the only wise thing to do was to turn southward and pick
up the Spanish Trail again. Captain Smith would not be persuaded but "swore by the gods he would go straight ahead, if he
died in the attempt."[34] They named the place where they separated "Division Spring," and the Mormon company under the
inspired leadership of General Rich headed south again for the
Spanish Trail.

Captain Smith and his men recklessly pursued the cutoff
route, but they soon became desperate for water. After killing a
horse and drinking its blood, the captain and all but eleven men
returned. These eleven men from Captain Smith's company

continued on the cutoff. Later, twenty of the 107 wagons from
Jefferson Hunt's wagon train caught up with them. The gold
seekers in these twenty wagons had gone against the wise counsel
of their guide and had decided to follow the packers on the cutoff route. The majority of this group lost their lives in the well-
known Death Valley tragedy.[35] Had it not been for Elder Rich, a
similar fate may well have befallen the young Mormon missionaries, and George Q. Cannon was swift to give the Lord credit
for inspiring Brother Rich to effect their escape: "I have always
thought that his presence [Brother Rich's] with us saved us from
many perils, and it is not too much to say that he was the means,
in the hands of the Lord, of saving our lives."[36]

General Rich's pack train soon caught up with Brother Hunt
and the wagons that had stayed with him on the Spanish Trail,
and these two groups traveled together. By this time the buckskin mare could no longer carry George. He had to dismount
and lead the spent horse. One time, because his horse was "so reduced in flesh," George walked across a fifty-mile stretch of
desert. He became violently ill from some bad water he drank, so
ill that he had to lie down several times and reached camp late in
the night. He remembered with dread that he had three hours of
guard duty to fill on his arrival at camp, but an unusual circumstance met him when he got there:

> Judge . . . of my surprise and gratitude when upon my arrival and
> making inquiry, I learned that General Rich had stood my guard!
> He thought I would be sufficiently fatigued, he said, after walking
> fifty miles, to need all the sleep I could get, without having to
> stand guard, so he had taken my place! Now, if I had been his
> equal in years or in other respects, this act of kindness might not,
> perhaps, have been worthy of any particular remark. . . . But Gen-
> eral Rich was one of the Twelve Apostles, the chief man in the

company, nearly old enough to be my father, while I was an obscure young man, just on the threshold of life, with nothing special about me to recommend me to his consideration and kindness but our common humanity. He was the last man in the company, because of the position he occupied, whom I would have looked for (if I had looked for any one) to have done me such a favor. You can imagine how much this kindness endeared him to me! It made an indelible impression upon me, which has been deepened and strengthened by acts of a similar character which I repeatedly witnessed during the long years of our subsequent intercourse.[37]

Part of the "subsequent intercourse" of which Brother Cannon speaks came when he served with Charles C. Rich on the Council of the Twelve Apostles and presided with him years later over the British Mission.

Finally George's horse was not even able to keep up with the wagons, and he had to turn her loose. The entry for Sunday, November 25, reads: "Today my mare gave out. I had to let her go without anything on her; my things carried by the brethren of the mess. I saved her as much as I possibly could having walked principally the whole way for fear of her failing."[38] The long walk had ruined his boots and also worn out his moccasins—he was barefooted when the snow began to fall. George became very ill and lay under a drafty shelter in the snow without food or means of transportation. The brethren shot and killed an owl for him, from which they made some warm broth. He said that it was "the nicest dish of soup I had ever tasted. . . . Sharp hunger makes food taste wonderfully sweet; a piece of a donkey or of a dog eats very well when one is very hungry. I know this for I have tried them both."[39]

Because George was not the only member of the company who was incapacitated, Brothers Rich and Hunt decided to divide the company, sending those who had strong animals ahead to send back help for the rest. George stayed with the laggers, who were soon met with provisions and supplies. Shortly afterward they reached Williams Ranch, where George again became ill, but he was able to rally before long and finished his journey northward past San Francisco to the goldfields of the American River.[40]

Digging Gold

In the goldfields, Elder Cannon found an anomalous environment for missionaries: evil and ungodliness reigned on every side. The corrupt men he associated with desired nothing more than to dig gold for six days and then repair to town to drink, gamble, dance, and fight. George hated this society, and in consequence he said, "I heartily despised the work of digging gold."[41] George had always refrained from drinking hard liquor, but here in California some "roughs" on one occasion forced some whiskey down the throat of the young missionary in spite of his struggle to resist.[42] Not only did the Word of Wisdom set this Mormon group apart from the other miners, but their attitude toward their findings was different: "When they [the Mormons] panned the black dust or the flakes that looked like bran or found the nuggets on their riffle boards, there was no wild exultation or hurry to go on a spending spree. They were digging the gold to send back to their brethren in Zion in the mountains."[43]

At one time George became so fed up with the gold digging business that he decided to take a job, offered to him because of his accounting experience, as manager of a trading post at $50.00 a day. He figured that the steadiness of this income would net him as much to send to the Church as the irregular, though sometimes more remunerative, days of gold mining. Even this occupation was tainted, however, because he had to sell whiskey to the miners—a task that was against his lofty principles. He soon gave up the post.[44]

For the fall of 1850, an interesting series of entries appears in his journal which illustrate the proceeds of a week's diggings. The first day reads: "Went to work this morning in the claim; prospects were very poor during the morning; but towards the close of the day struck it pretty rich." And on the next day: "Took it out pretty freely today." Three times he mentioned the exact amount of each miner's share after dividing the proceeds of the day's work: "$200 apiece," "$400 apiece," and "$92 apiece." About ten days later he recorded: "Worked until Tuesday night when the diggings failed."[45]

The biggest problem the missionaries faced seemed to be the rains, which virtually stopped the mining process. The following letter, dated September 26, from the pen of Elder Cannon to Joseph Caine, a resident in Great Salt Lake City, appeared in the *Deseret News*: "Saturday last it commenced raining and we were not able to do anything on the claim; Sunday was fine, and Monday the river had so raised, that work could not be done; but this night it descended in torrents without intermission all night; Tuesday evening (Sept. 24) the stream rose several feet in a few minutes; it carried everything before it with irresistible force; rockers, pumps, boards, etc., etc. floated past; from all accounts every dam on the river suffered."[46]

Associating with the miners was bad enough when they were busy, but it was terrible when they had no work to keep them occupied. George noted that when the waters caused the miners to stop working, in their idleness they would "gamble away what little they had; and those who had nothing, had nothing to do but steal, rob, play at cut-throat, and such like social games, hoping to get something to satisfy hunger. He reported that there were about five murders each day and that no one was safe. The law enforcement was practically nil. The prospect of spending a winter in such an atmosphere filled the young elder with gloom: "Many will probably go to the Sandwich Islands to winter; many will doubtless sicken and die, as others have done, leaving their wives, widows and their children, fatherless; and many more who can neither die, nor get away, nor get food sufficient, must in all probability, suffer exceedingly. Among the rich, genteel and refined, drinking and gambling, gambling and drinking are the popular exercises from morning to evening and from evening to morning, and this is the way great fortunes are lost and won."[47]

The same month that George wrote this dismal letter, his own prospects for the future began to brighten. The mission presidency, Elders Rich and Lyman, saw no benefit in having the young gold missionaries winter in California when the warm Sandwich Islands (now the Hawaiian Islands) were close and the people there were ignorant of the marvelous work the Lord had wrought in this day. The night before Brother Rich formally called George Q. Cannon and eight other men on missions to the Sandwich Islands, George wrote in his journal: "He [President Rich] had hinted to me that I would go to the Sandwich Islands for the winter as well as some other of the brethren. This evening he asked if I had any objections to going. I told him I was on hand to do whatever he thought best as Brother Young had told me upon leaving the Valley to obey the counsel of Bro. Amasa Lyman and Bro. Rich and I should be blessed."[48]

Henry W. Bigler, one of the other eight who were called, related in his journal the official call that came the next day:

> This morning Elder Chas. C. Rich called us together and said that he wanted some of us to go on a mission to the Sandwich Islands and stated that it was his opinion it would cost us no more to spend the winter there than it would here, for we could make nothing in the mines in the winter season, in consequence of so much water being in the streams, and provisions being so high in the mining camps it would cost us more to stay here and make nothing than it would if we went to the Islands . . . and [that was]the best counsel he could give, for we should, as it were, be killing two birds with one stone, for we could live as cheaply there and perform a mission at the same time. He then called on ten of us, one of whom was sent to go to Oregon, namely Bro. Boyd Steward, and the remaining nine were set apart for the islands as follows: Thomas Whittle, Thomas Morris, John Dixon, George Q. Cannon, William Farrer, John W. Berry, James Keeler, James Hawkins and myself, and he blessed us in the name of the Lord and told us to act as the Spirit directed after arriving at the Islands.[49]

All his life George had dreamed of being a missionary; now at last the Lord saw fit to make this his calling. Whether he faced the prospect with unmixed emotions is not known, but for him it was the beginning of a work he loved and whose value he longed to help others see. He once remarked: "I have thought that the missionary spirit did not burn as brightly in some of our young men as it should—that they did not understand the value of human souls in the sight of the Lord and the precious rewards which He bestows upon those who seek, in the proper way, to save them."[50]

Young George was surely one whose high ideals and devotion to the cause of righteousness had prepared him to obtain these great rewards. Elizabeth had said that she would rather he be "saving souls" than digging gold, and George himself no doubt recalled the childhood dream he had expressed to his young schoolmates in England, a dream that had intensified as he listened to the missionaries in Nauvoo—"No calling was so noble in my eyes as that of a standard-bearer of the gospel."[51] Now he could leave his task of digging gold in an environment which he felt was degrading and launch forth on that calling which he considered highest in life: preaching the gospel of Jesus Christ to his fellowmen.

CHAPTER 4

The Hawaiian Mission

Mission Preparations—Temporal and Spiritual

ON AN AUTUMN DAY IN October of 1850, in one of the beautiful canyons of the Sierra Nevada Mountains, Elder George Q. Cannon was set apart as a missionary of The Church of Jesus Christ of Latter-day Saints under the hands of Elder Charles C. Rich.[1] The next few weeks were busy ones for Elder Cannon and his companions as they prepared to set sail for their mission to the Sandwich Islands.

Part of Elder Cannon's preparation consisted of securing a few much-needed books from which to preach the gospel. He apparently did not even have a copy of the Book of Mormon to

Na-lima-nui, an early Hawaiian convert, ca. 1870

call his own; a journal entry records his gratitude to a Brother and Sister Cahoon for giving him a hymnal and a Book of Mormon before leaving: "I spoke about some books. I told our situation that we had none etc. She [Sister Cahoon] said she had a hymn book she would let me have and when Bro. Cahoon got back he might let me have a Book of Mormon. She invited me up to breakfast. I offered her a $5.00 gold piece for the hymn book but she would not take it. I left it laying on the table."[2] He succeeded in getting the Book of Mormon from Brother Cahoon by promising to bring him a souvenir from the Sandwich Islands.

Henry W. Bigler's diary records the names of the original nine missionaries who were called on September 25, 1850. One of them, John W. Berry, who "was called with discretionary power to go or not, as his circumstances would permit," did not accompany them.[3] However, two others were called—Hirum H. Blackwell and Hirum Clark—making a total of ten missionaries. In early November all the missionaries except Elder Clark proceeded from San Bernardino to San Francisco, their port of departure. While awaiting Elder Clark's arrival and the date of sailing, Elder Cannon had two revelatory dreams that demonstrated his penchant for this spiritual gift. In the first dream he witnessed Elder Clark's arrival in every detail several days before it occurred.[4] The other dream came to him after they boarded the ship *Imaum of Muscat* and while they were waiting for favorable winds to carry them out of the Bay. The dream left a deep and lasting impression on Elder Cannon, for he felt it was given from of the Lord to teach him to rely on prayer as he faced the many hardships of his mission ahead. In recounting this experience, Elder Cannon recalled:

There were ten of us, of whom I was the youngest, wind-bound in the Bay of San Francisco, and we had been thus delayed for nearly a week near the Golden Gate in consequence of head winds. I dreamed one night that this party of brethren were heaving at the windlass, having a rope attached to it reaching forward to the anchor at the bow of the vessel. We were working with all our might endeavoring to raise the anchor, but seemingly we made but little progress. While thus engaged I thought the Prophet Joseph came from the after part of the vessel dressed in his temple clothes, and tapping me on the shoulder told me to go with him. I went, and he climbed on to the forecastle and there he knelt down, also telling me to kneel down with him. He prayed according to the order of prayer which is revealed. After prayer, he arose upon his feet. "Now," said he, "George, take hold of that rope"—the rope we had been pulling on with all our might. I took hold of it, and with the greatest ease and without the least effort, the anchor was raised. "Now," said he, "let this be a lesson to you; remember that great things can be accomplished through the power of prayer and the exercise of faith in the right way."5

The power of prayer did help them on their voyage. The *Imaum of Muscat* was "an unseaworthy . . . vessel, and only through the intervention of a kind Providence were they saved from a watery grave."6 A perilous storm hit the first night at sea. Describing this terrible night, Elder Cannon recorded: "That night was one of great anxiety to the captain, officers and crew. We also realized that we were in a critical position, and exerted all the faith we could. The Captain had his wife with him, and so little hope did he have at one time of saving the vessel, that he told her to prepare for eternity, for he did not think we would ever see daylight in this world again."7

When morning came the storm abated, and all were joyful to have been spared. Elder Cannon felt that their special calling as missionaries had saved them: "In considering our narrow escape afterwards, we felt to give the glory of our deliverance to God. We were His servants, and on His business, and He had preserved us."[8]

The Voyage to Hawaii

This vessel was not only unseaworthy but also unworthy in a number of other ways. The missionaries' quarters between decks were extremely dark and low-ceilinged; the missionaries had to provide their own bedding, and the food was at the mere subsistence level. Originally the captain had promised to serve them "cabin fare," but Elder Cannon quipped, "Either this part of the contract was not fulfilled, or they lived poorly in the cabin."[9]

The elders also suffered another great discomfort; they were violently seasick from the first hours of their voyage. On one occasion, when all of them were using the one seasick bucket that had been provided for ten of them, George, the youngest member of the group, could not help seeing the humor of the situation and laughed aloud. This levity earned him a stern rebuke from one member of the group and frowns of disapproval from the rest.

After nearly a month at sea, on December 12, 1850 they caught sight of "the rough mountainous isles of the Hawaiian group." Anxious to end their unpleasant voyage, George penned, "We longed to tread upon them."[10] The weather-beaten hulls of several wrecked vessels clinging to the reefs around the island reminded them that they were not safe until they were anchored securely in the harbor. Even before they anchored, dozens of native Hawaiians boarded the ship to sell them trinkets and fresh tropical fruit. Elder Cannon described these "strange people": "The monotonous character of their language, their rapid utterance, their numerous gestures, caused us to watch them with interest. We thought them a strange people. I little thought at that time that I would ever learn their language, or become as familiar with their customs as I afterwards did; for, though we had been sent on missions to the Islands, we supposed our time would be occupied in preaching to the whites."[11]

And so on this winter day of 1850, ambassadors of the restored gospel of Christ set foot for the first time on the Hawaiian Islands. Seven years earlier four other elders (Noah Rogers, Addison Pratt, Benjamin F. Grouard, and Knowlton F. Hanks) had been called to these islands, but because the only boat on which they could book passage was going to the Society Islands they changed their field of labor and served their mission in the South Pacific rather than on the Sandwich Islands.[12]

The Work on the Islands Begins

One of the first things the missionaries did when they reached shore was ascend a nearby mountain, each carrying a stone, to erect a small altar at the top. There they sang a hymn and bore testimonies to one another; and Hirum Clark dedicated the land for the preaching of the gospel. One of the elders spoke in tongues and another interpreted his prophetic promises. They felt very close to the Lord. "The sun was sinking low in the heavens when we got through. Our descent was quickly made, for we felt joyful, and when men are joyful and the Spirit of God rests upon them, they feel lithe and active. We had been in the presence of the Lord, and had felt his power, and why should we not be happy?"[13]

The oldest member of the group, Hirum Clark, who had been appointed president of the mission, chose as his companion Thomas Whittle, and as their field of labor the Island of Oahu. There were four other major islands and eight missionaries; President Clark appointed four of the missionaries to be presiding elders and had them draw lots for their island assignments and for the order in which they would choose their companions. George was astonished at being chosen as one of the presiding elders, since he was the youngest of the party. He drew the Island of Maui and had first choice in selecting a companion.

He wrote in his journal for Saturday, December 14, 1850: "We cast lots for the first choice and it fell to me. . . . I was nonplused for a minute or two not knowing who to take; the spirit dictated to me very plainly to choose Br. Keeler, he said he was willing."[14] Elder Keeler later disclosed to his new companion that he had separated himself from the group and besought the Lord to inspire Elder Cannon to choose him. Elder Cannon also felt spiritual confirmation concerning his lot to labor on Maui, for when he had sailed past that island two days before, his "feelings were drawn toward that island," and he was impressed that he should be most successful laboring there.

President Clark later decided to keep Elder Morris in Honolulu, so Elder Morris's companion, Elder Bigler, decided that instead of going alone to the island they had drawn (Molokai), he would accompany Elders Cannon and Keeler to Maui. These three elders first acquired lodging in a "native house" made of grass that Elder Cannon described as having the appearance of a haystack.

It was in this little grass house that the three elders spent their first Christmas. George's journal for Christmas Day, 1850, recorded his melancholy reflections of the home and family he had left far behind so long ago: "Home all day occupied reading and studying. My thoughts naturally reverted to home and its attractions. Today would be a fete day there and I thought that some of the family would be expressing themselves, wondering where George is today. I do not remember spending Christmas Day so quietly."[15]

The rent for this "native house," four dollars a week, soon exhausted the missionaries' funds, and they were obliged to seek the hospitality of the people, as did the missionaries who traveled without purse or scrip in other lands. Brother Keeler felt impressed that they should visit a little old native lady, Na-lima-nui, who lived near them and had done their washing for them. Upon their making clear to her their situation in their broken native speech, she offered to let them live in her house and expressed her willingness to move out and go live with her daughter. Of this kindness Brother Cannon said: "My heart swelled within me and I could scarcely refrain from weeping. I blessed her. She said she would fix things today and tomorrow night. Come in."[16]

One of the first things Elder Cannon and his companions did when they reached the island of Maui was visit Mr. Bunker, the American consul, and request an invitation to meet the governor of the Islands. Elder Cannon made a practice thereafter of always going to the highest officials on the island where he wished to preach and establishing with them his purposes and bearing his testimony. The elders requested of the governor, James Young, the privilege of preaching in the palace, which was then vacant. Governor Young put them off with talk of having to clear it through the minister of the interior and did not seem disposed to help them in any way. Instead, he pointed out that they could preach out of doors as the Protestant missionaries had done at first. The day of this visit, Saturday, January 18, 1851, Brother Cannon wrote in his journal: "I felt to pray that he might live to be sorry for not letting us have the House, for I believe he has power in himself."[17]

Although the missionaries failed to secure the palace, they were granted permission to meet in a chapel in Lahaina, where most of the white residents of the island worshiped. The elders soon realized that "if we were to confine our labors to the whites, our mission to those islands would be a short one."[18] White people were in the minority on the islands, and those who were there showed very little interest in the gospel.

President Rich had not told the elders to preach to the natives, but neither had he instructed them not to do so. The elders now questioned whether their mission calling would be fulfilled when they had "warned" the white people of the islands. The rather primitive living conditions, the almost impossibly difficult language, along with the widespread lack of success and no doubt general homesickness produced among the missionaries talk of going home. In addition to these problems common to all the elders, Elder Whittle was further discouraged by his feelings of uselessness as a companion to President Clark, who dominated every situation, not even allowing the younger missionary opportunity to bear his testimony. In addition to Elder Whittle, Elders Dixon, Farrer, and Blackwell felt that they had accomplished all they had been called to do, and decided to return home. But Elder Cannon's feelings about not leaving the islands were most definite:

I did not conceal my feelings from [the other Elders]; I told them that I could not go home under existing circumstances, without feeling condemned. The Lord, in my opinion, I said, would hold me accountable for not doing my duty to that people, if I were to leave them; and the people might rise up in judgment against me at some future day, for not having given them the privilege of hearing the truth. My prayer was that the time might speedily come when all should know the Lord, and when His knowledge would cover the earth as the waters covered the deep; and I believed in uniting works and faith. It would sound badly for ten Elders to be sent out to the islands by Elder Charles C. Rich, one of the Twelve Apostles, to preach and to act as the Spirit and circumstances might dictate, and when we found there were not whites that would receive us, turn around and go home, and leave a whole nation to welter in ignorance, because he did not happen to tell us that we were to preach to them in their own tongue.[19]

Elders Keeler, Bigler, and Hawkins shared similar feelings, and Elder Farrer, upon hearing the determination of Elder Cannon to remain, was also persuaded to stay on. Elder Farrer's companion, John Dixon, still determined to depart, added to his list of reasons the fact that he was a bachelor and needed to return to Zion and secure a wife. He said he would gladly take a mission to Europe or any other place where the living conditions were above the level of those of the islands. (Neither his hope to marry nor his promise to go on another mission materialized, for he was killed in an Indian ambush not long after arriving home.[20])

Unfortunately, even Hirum Clark, the mission president, did not seem content with preaching the gospel in the islands to which he had been called. Although he had brought the first member into the Church on the Sandwich Islands by baptizing a sixteen-year-old boy—a native at that—Elder Clark was determined to go to another field of labor.[21] He and Elder Morris planned to go to the Marquesas Islands several hundred miles to the south and wanted the other five elders to go with them. Because Elder Clark was presiding over them, they faced a difficult decision. They clearly felt that they had been called to preach in the Sandwich Islands, and yet their president was urging them to abandon their field of labor and follow him to a place which had not been designated by the Twelve Apostles.

Elder Cannon's objections to going were threefold. First, he explained: "I considered that I would have been just as much justified in leaving the first day as I would now; that we had not given the people a trial whether they would receive it [the gospel] or reject it."[22] He couched his second objection in these words: "I have no authority to go to Marquesas; if I had done my duty here and no more could be done and the people would not accept the truth my first proceeding should be start for home and report myself as having fulfilled my mission." His strongest objection, however, seemed to be that the Spirit, which Elder Rich had told them should direct them, bade him to stay: "In fact every time I had prayed to the Lord that there might be a good work done here I felt warm and felt the spirit continually whispering to me if I should persevere I should be blest, and to leave with these feelings would be for me to go directly in opposition to the manifestations of the spirit to me."[23]

Elder Cannon went to Na-lima-nui's garden to pray, there beseeching the Lord, perhaps more ardently than he ever had before in his life, to tell him what to do. His prayer was answered by a marvelous manifestation: "It was here that he talked with the Lord, heard His voice and felt His holy presence. This was such a sacred experience that he seldom made any public reference to it. It remained with him all his life. His dying testimony to his son who sat by his bedside in his last hours was that he knew that God lived, for he had heard His voice."[24]

President Clark, seeing that Elder Cannon and his four companions were determined to remain, agreed that it would be better for them to stay on the Sandwich Islands until they were satisfied that they had warned the people sufficiently. The "Manuscript History of the Hawaiian Mission" gives the following synopsis of Elder Clark's fate: "Elder Clark deserted his mission February 22, 1851, and sailed for the Society Islands. He finally landed in California, where he committed suicide."[25]

When Brigham Young heard of the many elders who had deserted their missions in the Islands, he wrote to Elder Cannon, commending him for his loyalty: "We were well pleased with the course you had taken and the conclusions which the brethren and yourself had come to, in reference to remaining in the Islands until you had laid a foundation agreeable to your instructions from Elder C. C. Rich. It has been our constant prayer to our Heavenly Father that you might be blest and prospered."[26] The Church leaders evidently believed that "a foundation" could be laid, because from time to time they sent additional missionaries to assist the remaining elders and to replace those who had defected.

Now that the five faithful Elders remained, they were free to give their full attention to the challenge of preaching the gospel to the native Hawaiians. Elder Cannon's knowledge that the natives to whom he was preaching were members of the house of Israel and heirs to the same promises made to the Lamanites in the Book of Mormon spurred him on in the work: "If the sons of Mosiah could relinquish their high estate, and go forth among the degraded Lamanites to labor as they did, should not I labor with patience and devoted zeal for the salvation of these poor red men, heirs of the same promise?"[27]

Elder Cannon realized that these people were sons and

daughters of God, as dear to Him as any of His children: "The soul of a Sandwich Islander or a Lamanite is as precious in the sight of the Lord as the soul of white man, whether born in America or Europe. Jesus died for one as much as the other, and to the men of red skins the Lord's promises are great and precious. Those who administer the ordinances of salvation to them will have fully as great joy over them in the day of the Lord Jesus as if they had been more enlightened."[28]

Learning the Hawaiian Tongue

The elders' first consideration in carrying the gospel to the natives was to learn the Hawaiian tongue. "They went up into the mountain behind Lahaina, Maui, and fasted and prayed all day that the Lord would aid them in learning the language and would help them to touch the hearts of the natives with the gospel message."[29] After months of struggling, Elder Cannon received a miraculous blessing from the Lord to help him learn the language. He joyously recorded in a letter to his Aunt Leonora:

My desire to learn to speak was very strong; it was present with me night and day and I never permitted an opportunity of talking with the natives to pass without improving it. I also tried to exercise faith before the Lord to obtain the gift of talking and understanding the language. One evening, while sitting on the mats conversing with some neighbors who had dropped in, I felt an uncommonly great desire to understand what they said. All at once I felt a peculiar sensation in my ears, I jumped to my feet, with my hands at the sides of my head, and exclaimed to Elders Bigler and Keeler, who sat at the table, that I believed I had received the gift of interpretation! And it was so. From that time forward I had but little, if any, difficulty in understanding what the people said.

I might not be able at once to separate every word which they spoke from every other word in the sentence; but I could tell the general meaning of the whole. This was a great aid to me in learning to speak the language, and I felt very thankful for this gift from the Lord.[30]

With this divine aid, Elder Cannon gained exceptional fluency in the language. He worked very hard to build his language ability by not reading any books in English except the Book of Mormon and the Doctrine and Covenants. "Of course it required an effort on my part to thus train myself; but I was paid for it all in the fluency with which I used the language. I was able to speak and write it with greater ease and correctness than my mother tongue."[31]

Once when he was asked to speak to a group of white people on the islands, he explained this phenomenon of finding it easier to speak Hawaiian than English: "Yesterday, Sunday, 24th, I preached to a white congregation; I had a good flow of the Spirit; but still it is a fact though I would not have credited it if I had been told so some time ago, that it is a great deal easier for me to speak or pray in native than in my mother tongue; not that I can express my ideas with as much force, probably, as I can in my native tongue, but I have been accustomed to using native almost entirely, and therefore my thoughts and ideas naturally seek vent in that channel, and I can speak with greater freedom."[32]

Because of this proficiency, "there was a general call from all quarters for Brother Cannon to come and preach to them as he understood the language."[33] Elder Cannon never failed to acknowledge the source of this marvelous gift. In a letter to his Aunt Leonora he attributed this blessing from the Lord to the prayers of his loved ones: "I have been told repeatedly that there never has been a missionary [referring to Protestant and Catholic missionaries too] upon these islands that has been anything like as forward as I am in the language for the time I have been upon the islands; in fact it is very visible to me that the Lord has blessed me extraordinarily. Why is it so? Is it because of myself or my prayers? No; in a small degree, perhaps; but I feel to give you the credit for it, that live at home, for your prayers."[34]

Translating the Book of Mormon into Hawaiian

In January 1852, only one year after Elder Cannon's arrival on the islands, he commenced the monumental task of translating the Book of Mormon into native Hawaiian—one of the greatest and most far-reaching contributions of Elder Cannon's entire mission. When the First Presidency of the Church learned of this effort, Brother Cannon was encouraged by receiving from "Presidents Young, Kimball and Richards words of cheer, approving of what I was doing and counseling me to persevere."[35]

In March of the previous year, in the city Wailuku, Elder Cannon had met Judge Jonata Napela, who became a great friend and the best help he ever received on the translation of the Book of Mormon: "Probably few in the nation were as well qualified as Brother Napela, to help me in this respect. He was a descendant of the old chiefs of the Island of Maui, in whose families the language was preserved and spoken in the greatest purity."[36] His native friend's knowledge of both the language and the gospel made him invaluable in the work. Elder Cannon was affected greatly by working so closely with the scriptures: "I never could enter into the feelings experienced by the holy men who wrote the Book of Mormon, as I can at present; my soul shrinks from the thought of sin and my heart is pained to behold the sins of the world. I can weep over the weakness, folly and shortsightedness of man."[37]

Evidently, translating the scriptures had much the same effect on Brother Napela. Elder Cannon wrote of him: "As I progressed with the translation, his comprehension of the work increased. He got the spirit of the book and was able to seize very quickly the points presented to him."[38]

After the first translation was completed, Brother Cannon did not cease his labors until he went through the whole of it again with the help of another native resident, Kauwahi, who lived on the farthermost west of the islands at Waimea, Kauai. This man was said to be "a man of acute intellect and talent and good education, and who was called the most eloquent and best reasoner in the Hawaiian nation."[39] Elder Cannon recorded in his journal for December 24, 1853: "Commenced reading the translation of the Book of Mormon in company with Bros. Farrer and Kauwahi for the purpose of correcting any inaccuracies that might be in the translation and to see that no words or sentences had been left out."[40]

The work was ready for publication exactly three years after it was begun. Brother Karren, a missionary who had joined them on the islands, after reporting earlier in his journal that "they were progressing tolerably well in the work of revising the manuscript of the Book of Mormon," wrote on January 31, 1854, "Elders George Q. Cannon and William Farrer finished their revision of the Book of Mormon at Waimea, Kauai."[41] Already Elder Cannon had begun making preparations for printing the book. In November 1853, "upon mature deliberation in conference," they decided that because of the extremely high cost of printing on the islands, and also because one of the most likely printers had refused to publish the book because of its connection with the Mormon Church, they should purchase a press and type and have them sent from New York to the islands. The Hawaiian members bought copies of the book in advance to pay for the press. Elder Cannon admitted that "it appears like a large undertaking, looking at it naturally among so poor a people, yet we all felt that we would be blessed of the Lord in attempting it."[42] Because Elder Cannon returned to the mainland before the press arrived, the press was sent to San Francisco, where, during his third mission (to be discussed in another chapter), he completed the publication of these scriptures that were so helpful in converting and sustaining the Saints on the faraway Sandwich Islands.

Missionary Experiences Among the Natives

Once the missionaries had decided to labor with earnestness among the native people, the elders began to enjoy success from their labors. In March 1851 Elder Hawkins baptized six and later eight Hawaiians, and in April, fourteen more.[43] The other elders enjoyed similar accomplishments, and in August 1851 "Elders Cannon and Keeler administered the sacrament to 190 members of the Church at Honamanu and baptized fifteen new converts."[44] In a letter to his Aunt Leonora, Elder Cannon reported even greater success within the following week: "At Keanae, in four days there were 131 baptized and confirmed into the Church."[45] Elder Cannon saw the fulfillment of a prophecy in this success: "I have been reminded frequently of Uncle's blessing upon my head while living in the valley—that I should stand in the waters as the Savior, and call upon the multitudes to come forward and be baptized."[46]

Because in some parts of the Islands the natives saw so few

white people, the elders were seen as a great oddity. The missionaries capitalized on this attention, of course. Elder Cannon wrote: "Our appearance was generally hailed by the cry of "the white men," and troops of boys and girls, as well as grown up natives, rushed to the road side to scrutinize us, and ask questions, which gave us a good opportunity to lay our principles, to some small extent, before them, which were productive of some good."[47]

Before long the elders found themselves very fond of these friendly and lovable people. One of the missionaries described them this way: "We feel sanguine that this people are of the Covenant blood, and that a great work is to be done among them. Many of them are quick of apprehension, and are apt to believe the truth. They are naturally an honest, and kindhearted people."[48] Elder Farrer also pointed out the outstanding qualities of kindness and generosity among the Hawaiian people: "The natives are a kindhearted people and will do all they can to make a missionary comfortable; they will give the last mouthful of food, the best and only bed; and if one's legs are weary through walking, they will lomi (rub) them and take the soreness out."[49]

Elder Cannon's journal contains many incidents that bespeak this kindness toward him and the other elders. The natives were more than willing to give what they had, however little, when they discovered that the elders had even less. David Malo, "one of the best informed men on the island," approached Elder Cannon, who was leaving on a journey: "This morning before starting, David presented me with 37 1/2 cents to buy water if I should need it. I did not want to take it. He pressed me and I accepted it. He had understood from me the evening before the way we traveled. I felt to bless the old gentleman for his kindness to me."[50]

On another occasion, Elder Cannon and his companion were transferring their field of labor to another island. A member of the Church had given the missionaries a letter of introduction to one of his relatives who lived on the island where they were going in hopes that this relative would offer his hospitality to the homeless elders. The letter "did not have the least effect, however, on this churl; all he desired apparently was to obtain money, and his demeanor disgusted us."[51] Another young native who witnessed the unkindness of this man approached the elders hesitantly. Inviting them to come to his home, he said, "the aloha (love) has sprung up in my heart for you." Of this experience, Elder Cannon remarked, "This young man although a perfect stranger, kindly and hospitably opened his house to us, furnished us with food, killed a pig for us to eat and did everything in his power to make us comfortable, and the next morning insisted on accompanying us as a guide to the volcano; yet for all this kindness he would accept no pay in return."[52]

This young man's affinity for the elders extended also to their message, and he was soon baptized, along with a number of his neighbors.

When the Spirit of the Lord reached these people, who were already so good, they became dedicated members of the Church and made many sacrifices to build up the kingdom, including the donation of means and labor to build chapels. On September 1, 1852, Elder Cannon recorded: "The meeting house built by the brethren here is an excellent one and excels the Calvinistic meeting house; it is the best of any we have built."[53] Because the population of the Church was increasing so fast, many more meetinghouses were needed. In order to facilitate this construction, Elder Cannon "had some idea of teaching them the principle of tithing, but wished to get the mind of the spirit in regard to it—and if right, that we might be sustained in teaching it, and that their hearts might be prepared to receive it. . . . We went to a retired place and offered up our prayers to our Father—that we might be blessed and we did realize and feel that it was right to teach it and that they would be prepared."[54]

The hesitancy the missionaries felt in regard to introducing tithing to the natives was a consequence not only of the poverty but also of the fact that Protestant missionaries for many years had made themselves burdensome by soliciting funds for their own support. Reinforced by the Spirit, Elder Cannon presented himself before a congregation of members who were struggling to commence work on their chapel. "I arose and cited to them our prosperity as a people and also the cause and went on to explain the principle of tithing from the scriptures and was blessed with a powerful share of the spirit. They felt it and were melted down; several of them spoke and felt glory in it."[55]

The great dedication of the natives served as an example and an encouragement even to Brother Cannon, as he indicated by his reflections at the death of one of these faithful Saints:

Tokorren is dead; it was with sorrow that I heard this news as I had learned to love Bro. Tok. He was a young man but from the time of his joining the Church he had been indefatigable in his exertions, completely devoted to the work, sparing no pains to magnify his Priesthood. His influence was great and he was a son of thunder. His death was a sudden one supposed to have been brought on by exposure. The day before he died he preached an hour and a half. He has gone to reap the reward of his labors and I pray that when the Lord sees fit to call me home, it will be in a time when I am wholly in His service and I know that this may be the case. I must always be devoted to His cause.[56]

One of the closest friends Elder Cannon made on his mission was the educated native judge Jonata H. Napela, who helped him with the translation of the Book of Mormon. Early in his mission, in March 1851, he had decided to leave Na-lima-nui's house for a time and venture forth to a town called Wailuku. He began his journey before breakfast that morning, and when wading across a river he slipped and fell down, making himself somewhat unpresentable. Not wanting to let his appearance deter him, he went on into the town to begin his work. However, he was too embarrassed to call on anyone because of the indelicacy of "going in and introducing myself in the plight I was in."[57] He determined to return home to change his clothes, but he reported that when he reached the outskirts of the village "I . . . felt impressed to return into town. I turned down into town and when passing a house, there were some men standing at the gate. I saluted them and passed on. I got a few hundred yards when they called me back, asked me to go in, and asked me where I was going. I told them I had thought of returning to Lahaina on account of the weather. One of them said I better stop until Monday with him."[58]

The man who extended this hospitality was Judge Napela; Brother Cannon stayed in his home and eventually succeeded in bringing into the Church not only him but also other members of his household and many of his friends. After one month's residence there, Elder Cannon felt that his presence in the house was the cause of some dissension. The Protestant missionaries and their families, as well as Napela's wife, were opposed to the Mormon and his work. In order to spare the judge any further trouble, he decided to return to Lahaina. The next day he started back. Before he left, Napela said that as soon as things were right he should come back.

He did return to Judge Napela's for a time, but again persecutions were so strong that the judge himself hinted it might be best for Elder Cannon to leave them: "Mr. Napela informed me today that Mr. Conde [one of the Protestant missionaries] had told the whole congregation that if he did not turn me out he should turn him out of the church. Napela informed me of this and at the same time told me he did not want to quarrel with the [Protestant] missionaries; it was a kind of round about way of telling me to leave in the morning."[59]

From here Elder Cannon went to Kulu, and he did not return to Wailuku for many months. In December of 1851 he and his companion, Elder Hammond, wanted to return to Napela's house. But Elder Cannon "felt somewhat delicate about going to Napela's after leaving his house under the circumstances that I did." They sought the Lord's guidance and were impressed that they should return there. They received a warm welcome and became engaged in a gospel conversation with Napela and some of his friends, which lasted "until the roosters crowed for morning."[60] One of these friends was Kamakau, "a member of Parliament and said to be one of the smartest natives on the islands." Brother Napela's account of his own association with Elder Cannon demonstrates the great effect this young missionary had on the judge's life and on his testimony of the gospel. This inspiring letter was written in native language to Brigham Young and translated for publication in the *Deseret News:*

In the year 1851, in the month of March, the fifth day, George Cannon came into my house at Wailuku, the Island of Maui, of the Hawaiian group. He was afterwards persecuted by our former teacher, D. T. Conde; therefore, George Cannon went from my house to Kulu, upon this Island. He afterwards established a

branch of the Church of the Lord there; and when the last month
of that year arrived, George Cannon and (Bro.) Hammond established a branch of the church of the Lord at Wailuku, and when
the year 1852 arrived, it had increased, and it is constantly increasing at this time; and it is very plain to us that this is the
Church of God, and that it is the gospel which is preached by the
white men from the Rocky Mountains; and there are many upon
these islands who have obtained strong faith by the grace of God,
through Jesus Christ, the Lord, that we might receive the Holy
Ghost; Amen.[61]

Hardships and Obstacles on the Islands

Brother Cannon's willingness to suffer the privations and
hardships of Hawaiian life in order to establish the kingdom
there was a source of inspiration to many other missionaries, including Joseph F. Smith, who at age fifteen reached the islands
shortly after George's departure. In a conference address given
thirty years after his mission, when he was serving in the First
Presidency with George Q. Cannon, President Smith comtrasted
President Cannon's willingness to sacrifice to another man's dis-
dainful attitude:

Soon after I was sent, there was a very bright, intelligent man
called to go to the Islands, and it was one of the causes of his
apostasy. "What," said he, "Send me, a linguist, a man well read,
an educated man, and an Englishman at that, to preach to hea-
thens?". . . . When Brother George Q. Cannon was called to go to
the Islands, he had no such feelings. He learned the language and
translated the Book of Mormon into the Hawaiian language. He
performed a glorious mission, and is now one of the First Presidency of the Church. And singular as it may appear, out of the

number of Elders that have been on missions to the Sandwich Islands, I can count more Apostles, more Presidents of Stakes, Bishops and leading men, than can be found in the same number that have gone to any other country. Why is this? Perhaps it is because they manifested their willingness to descend below all things, that they might rise above all things. If a man in the Church would be exalted, let him humble himself; and he that would exalt himself, God will abase.[62]

One of the hardships Elder Cannon endured was adjusting to the native diet, which consisted mainly of poi, a substance made from a grain called kalo. He related this incident, both amusing and inspiring, in regard to this food which was so repulsive to him at first:

> I had tasted a teaspoonful of "poi" but the smell of it and the calabash in which it was contained was so much like that of a bookbinder's old, sour, paste pot that when I put it to my mouth I gagged at it, and would have vomited had I swallowed it. But in traveling among the people, I soon learned that if I did not eat "poi" I would put them to great inconvenience; for they would have to cook separate food for me every meal. This would make me burdensome to them, and might interfere with my success. I, therefore, determined to learn to live on their food, and that I might do so, I asked the Lord to make it sweet to me. My prayer was heard and answered; the next time I tasted it, I ate a bowlful, and I positively liked it. It was my food, whenever I could get it from that time as long as I remained on the islands.[63]

When Elder Cannon recalled the owl soup he ate in the snowstorm of the Spanish Trail, he also mentioned another memorable meat dish he tasted on his mission—donkey meat.

The natives of the Sandwich Islands served "jack-ass" to Elder
Cannon, who was surprisingly pleased at its palatability. Brother
Cannon and his companion stopped at the home of someone
they knew who "had a jack-ass cooked; it had fallen down a
precipice and been killed, and they ate it with excellent gusto,
saying that it excelled horse meat as much as horse meat excelled
beef. Beef they said was very strong and not near as sweet as
horse or ass. We had the curiosity to try it. Brother H. said he
would have recognized it very readily as not being anything he
had ever ate, but I feel pretty certain that if nothing had been
said about it, and it had been set before me to eat, that I would
have eaten it without having the least suspicion that it was anything of that kind; it was very tender and not at all lean."[64]

Besides owl and donkey, Elder Cannon also referred to having tried dog meat. The natives were very fond of eating a certain kind of dog that evidently is not known on the mainland.
The natives took great delight in relating to Elder Cannon how
they had fooled some squeamish American merchants into eating
dog meat by switching the head of a cooked pig with that of the
dog. The merchants would not touch the pork bearing the dog's
head, but ate with relish dog meat and would not afterward believe they had eaten dog until the natives made them examine the
bones for proof. Elder Cannon said that were it not for the prejudice, dog meat—the kind they had, cooked the way they did
it—would be "very sweet and tender."[65]

Food, however, was not really important to Brother Cannon.
He was one who qualified for the Savior's promise that he who
hungers and thirsts after righteousness will be filled with the
Spirit. He summed up his feelings this way: "But what I lacked
in food the Lord made up to me in the goodly degree of his
Spirit which he bestowed upon me. What I had to eat was a mat-

ter of indifference to me. I was happy, and I rejoiced as I never had before. Dreams, visions and revelations were given to me, and the communion of the Spirit was most sweet and delicious."[66]

Besides this strange diet, another physical hardship the missionaries were obliged to endure was the strenuous task of getting from one place to another. Elder Cannon never overcame his tendency to become acutely ill at sea, and whenever he voyaged from one island to another he was plagued with this unpleasant affliction. On the islands he usually had to walk long distances from one town to another, and this was often an exhausting test of his physical endurance. His journal entry for Sunday, February 6, 1853, illustrates how little a point he made of having to walk ten hours in a single day: "Started about 4 o'clock a.m. for Kula and arrived there a little after 9; I was tired and hungry and my feet were blistered. Had a good attendance, I preached and was blessed. Baptized three during intermission. Had Lord's supper in afternoon and had a very good meeting. Ate dinner and then started on foot to make my way. I arrived there at dusk, my feet very sore. Found all well."[67]

Another obstacle the elders encountered was the almost constant harassment of the missionaries from other churches. In a letter printed in the *Millennial Star*, Elder Cannon described the situation: "The missionaries, both Catholic and Protestant, are zealously engaged in endeavoring to retard the progress of truth by all the means in their power; but despite their opposition, it does and will continue to roll."[68] These missionaries had come to the islands more than thirty years earlier and were well established when the unprofessional Mormon preachers arrived. There seems to have been a great deal of jealousy among these various sects, who were granted favors from the government: "If one gets a piece of land from the government, and the other gets none, then there is a row commenced; they will call each other all the names they can lay their tongues to; but they are all rich, with good houses and large tracts of land, and that the very choicest, with plenty of cattle and horses, and everything to make themselves comfortable. A good share of the old stock which came out first, have taken offices under government, having thrown aside their Bible for the law book."[69]

It seems that very soon after the elders arrived, this spirit of contention was directed toward the Mormons. As early as June 1851, in a general meeting held in Honolulu, a leader of one of the prominent sects exclaimed: "Mormonism—this false religion has found its way into this part of the world, and obtained a few followers. Though probably no permanent ones."[70] These ministers even went so far as to persuade the landowners to use their influence to get the law officers to threaten the people with arrest for listening to the Mormons. These officers told the people they would bind them and take them into the courts of Lahaina or Honolulu if they continued to attend the meetings. Using the law to back their persecution was completely illegal, and the Mormon elders "sent Brother Cannon to the government to obtain papers stating that we had as good a right to preach our principles as the missionaries had to preach theirs."[71] Elder Cannon did not succeed in securing any such affidavits because Governor Young insisted "that the laws were sufficiently ample to protect us without anything further."[72] Fortunately, because the non-Mormon missionaries knew this form of persecution was illegal, it was never carried very far and eventually died out completely.

The great success the Mormon elders enjoyed so soon after their arrival quickly became a threat to the ministers of other religions and a source of jealousy—partly because they themselves had experienced relatively little success in converting either foreigners or natives: "They have seen their best days upon these islands, their power begins to wane; they are in great trouble about Mormonism. We have baptized some six or seven foreigners, which is a hard stick for them, they having never done the like upon the islands after a thirty years' residence here."[73]

The Mormons were also more successful than the Protestants and Catholics in persuading the natives to abandon their traditional practice of idolatry, which was still widespread. Although the non-Mormon missionaries had it made illegal, they had little effect in actually curbing this evil. Elder Cannon described this custom and suggested the reason for the missionaries' failure to turn the people from it: "The [non-Mormon] missionaries have been here thirty-one years; but notwithstanding all their efforts, they have not been able to extirpate idolatry, (how it can be expected though, as the system they teach is but idolatry); it is still prevalent, though done slyly, as it is breaking the law; and we have baptized several who have told us they have done it. The most common is the worship of the spirits of departed friends; but they also worship hogs, dogs, and cocks."[74]

The jealousy the missionaries of other faiths felt as a result of these Mormon successes made them "double their diligence to stop the progress of this 'wild delusion.'"[75] These attempts by these other missionaries were not entirely unsuccessful, as Elder Cannon indicated:

I felt impressed to go from there (Kulu) to Keanae. . . . My impressions were correct. The people of Keanae were in great trouble. They had been assailed by enemies from every side, and those who were weak in the faith were in perplexity. Some had

turned away, not being able to withstand the pressure. The Pres-
byterian missionary of that district had been there, and had done
all in his power to blacken our characters, to deride our doctrines
and to persuade the people to forsake the Church. Two French-
men, Catholic priests, had also been there, and they had done all
in their power to frighten the people from the truth. . . . It seemed
as if the devil had set all his agencies into operation to destroy the
work of God, and they told all the lies that could be brought to
bear against us.[76]

One of the most venomous anti-Mormons was the Presby-
terian minister Reverend D. T. Conde, already mentioned in
Napela's letter. On Sunday, March 31, 1851, Elder Cannon witnessed one of Conde's noxious attacks on the restored Church.
He raved to his congregation about the alleged delusions of
Joseph Smith and his "notoriously bad character"; he declared
that the Saints had risen up in rebellion and killed Joseph Smith
because of his wickedness and that Joseph's death was just pun-
ishment from God for the many sins the prophet had committed. At the conclusion of this tirade, Elder Cannon stepped forward and "told him I wanted to give him correct information
regarding the things he had told the people that morning, that
he might remove the effects of the lies which he had repeated to
them; for, I said, they were base lies and I was a living witness
that they were. . . . I bore him a solemn testimony respecting the
Prophet Joseph, and the truth of the work, and said I would
stand as a witness against him at the judgment seat of God."[77]

Because this happened early in his mission, Elder Cannon
was forced to give this valiant defense in English, which only
Conde and two of the congregation understood. Recalling the
experiences of the day, he vented his anguish in his journal that
evening: "My feelings while listening to this tirade can be better

imagined than described. I felt and thought if I owned the world, I should have given it to have been able to talk native. . . . Our conversation lasted about half an hour. I talked very fast for I was considerably excited and could scarcely command my feelings. They had been so much hurt listening to his slanders. . . . When I got back to Mr. N's house [Napela's] I could not refrain from weeping. I wept like a whipped child."[78]

If any good came from Conde's attack, perhaps it was in the powerful motivation that it gave Elder Cannon to continue striving to master the language.

The Gospel Progresses on the Islands

Elder Cannon later recorded in his journal many very successful defenses of the gospel given in Hawaiian. He told about a Mr. Bailey, who attempted to abuse the elders verbally: "He intended I believe to out talk us and browbeat us, but in this he was very much disappointed notwithstanding all his impudence and insulting remarks; we proved the saying of the Lord to be true to his servants 'that he would give them a mouth and wisdom. That all their adversaries could not gainsay nor resist.' I bore a powerful testimony to him of the truth of the work. He called me a bold man some three times during the conversation."[79]

Although the elders were very successful in using the scriptures to point out the truth of Mormonism, the Protestant missionaries rebelled at this all *too* convincing method. A letter from William Perkins, one of the Latter-day Saint missionaries, to Elder Charles C. Rich contains this account: "There are many persons here who talk against us, but they dare not test their belief with the Bible. The brethren (that is Cannon and Lewis)

called on missionary Baldwin by name; they put it to him so
hard that he ran out of the house like a dog who got hot water
on his tail and left the boys sitting. The boys [elders] sent word
to the missionaries [Protestant] that they would like to have the
missionaries call a meeting and have judges to decide whether
their faith was according to the Bible and see if the missionaries
faith would stand the test. They said they did not think it would
be right."[80]

On another occasion Elder Cannon was suffering from a
cold that had settled in his lungs, making him very hoarse. While
returning home from church, he met a Catholic priest who questioned him as to which church was the oldest. Although he had
just spoken in the Sunday meeting with great difficulty, he was
miraculously able to engage in "an argument which lasted from
one to two hours." He recorded: "I endeavored to get him to
take some plan and to answer me some questions as I said the
way we are doing is not going to result in anything; but this he
would not do, and it was very plain to be seen that he did not
wish any comparisons made between his church and the scriptures; the native spectators had several laughs at his expense. The
Lord blessed me with fluency in the language and I was enabled
to speak plainly, although after we parted I could scarcely speak
in consequence of the effect of the cold on my lungs."[81]

In the fall of 1852, nine new elders arrived from Great Salt
Lake City to bolster the proselytizing activity on the islands.
They brought with them a copy of the revelation on celestial or
plural marriage that had been given to the Prophet Joseph Smith
in Nauvoo (see Doctrine and Covenants 132). Apparently this
was the first time Elder Cannon had seen the revelation, since it
had just been made public.[82] He realized that this doctrine
would soon become added fuel for the fires of opposition on the

islands, so rather than waiting to combat the attacks that would be made, he engaged in some preventive preaching: "I preached on the doctrine of plurality and was blessed very much with the spirit and the people listened very attentively; we thought it best to do this to prevent the influence of lies etc. that we knew would certainly be used and also newspaper stories, and we felt that the best way to counteract the influence of false doctrine was to declare the truth to explain it fully to them that there might be no room for mistake or wickedness."[83]

Elder Cannon made very clear to the natives that the doctrine of polygamy was not to be practiced in the islands at that time: "I impressed very much upon them the necessity of not meddling with these things, that at present these things were not for them. I then read the revelation and explained every thing that I thought might be mysterious to them. The people felt well and enjoyed the spirit much."[84]

The fact that Elder Cannon was so successful in making the people feel good about such a difficult doctrine as polygamy indicates his power as a speaker. During his mission he carried out the promise he made upon accepting the higher priesthood that he would "with the help of the Lord" always speak and not try to excuse himself. His journal indicates, however, that his fear of speaking did not entirely leave him: "This morning . . . I spoke and had a good flow of the spirit. Since I left Wailuku I have experienced more feelings of fear and trepidation when meeting time is near than I have for sometime before, but yet the Lord has been with me and I have enjoyed his Spirit much."[85]

People all over the islands hailed Elder Cannon as a powerful and engaging speaker, and for years after he went home, whenever they heard anyone preach well they would exclaim, "He speaks like Cannon!"[86] Though many complimented him on his speaking ability, he never forgot the source of his power—the Holy Ghost. In his journal for Sunday, May 30, 1852, he expressed his gratitude not only for having the Spirit, but for losing it occasionally:

> We met under a very large Kukui tree which afforded a delightful shade and had a beautiful day although it rained on all sides of us. I preached in the forenoon and commenced with an excellent flow of the spirit, but afterwards lost it and I had consequently a hard time. I desired to come up here and give them a good preach, but the Lord saw fit to humble me and I felt to be chastened under his hand for I realized that if I should be blest and obtain everything that I wanted that I should be lifted up and this would probably be the cause of my destruction. By being left to myself occasionally, I realized the source from which all my strength proceeded.[87]

Because of his great appreciation of the Spirit, Elder Cannon wanted to teach the natives to be guided by it not only in their personal lives but also in the proceedings of every meeting. He described one of these meetings in which the Spirit was leading them:

> We met at half past ten and I spoke and then gave liberty to the Saints to do as the spirit dictated, sing, pray, speak, etc. and there was some excellent speaking done by the brethren and also singing and prayer. Our hearts were melted down and we were filled to overflowing, scarcely a person in the house who did not shed tears of joy. I sat and listened with great pleasure to the brethren's testimonies and felt edified with their remarks. Our meeting lasted about six hours and none seemed to be fatigued and when I arose to dismiss the meeting there was as much desire manifested by the saints to hear more as though the meeting had just commenced.[88]

pray to God. I thought upon hearing this dream that the Lord had answered his prayer and had given him plain manifestation of the true Church."[95]

After a meeting held at Waiehu, three persons approached Elder Cannon and asked him to administer to them. One of them was a blind man: "He had been blind for upwards of thirty years, but he began to mend from the time hands were laid upon him, and the next morning, he was able to see."[96] In his journal that evening, Elder Cannon wrote, "I was so full that language was too faint to attempt to describe my feelings. I could not talk."[97]

Leaving a Legacy on the Islands

Elder Cannon truly lost himself in the service of the Lord and his fellowman. He was completely involved in his mission among the good people of the Sandwich Islands, but he had been away from his home in the Great Salt Lake Valley for nearly five years. In a letter to his family, he made it clear that though he loved his work, he was very attached to his home: "I have written thus far without scarcely an allusion to home, or to all the folks there; but do not imagine that I am weaned; I am not the least, and the Lord forbid that I should; for I think that were I deprived of my love for home and its attractions, I would be deprived of the mainspring of my existence, and this world would be but a dreary waste—a blank."[98]

Although his journals make very few references to his sweetheart, Elizabeth, she was never far from his thoughts. The two had agreed to marry when he returned to the valley. Receiving a treasured letter from her, he recorded: "I felt good in receiving it as I have looked long and anxiously to get a letter from her; she

expressed her love in affectionate terms and looks with anxiety
for my return."[99] At one time Elizabeth wondered if he would
ever return home. Elder Cannon recorded: "The mail arrived
today from the valley bringing me three letters: one was from
Elizabeth which was very cheering and filled, as usual, with expressions of love and enduring affection. She is anxious to learn
of my return and says that some tell her that I am not coming
home, if she could think so, she says she would feel like shoul-
dering her pack and coming to meet me. Bless her, O Lord, for
her constancy and may she be strengthened continually and kept
unto the end."[100]

Elizabeth's desires for George's return were finally realized.
In the spring of 1854 word came from the brethren in Salt Lake
City that Elder Cannon and his four original companions were
free to return home. They continued to labor until July of that
year, when at last he prepared to board the ship at Honolulu.
The elders would not have been able to return even then had it
not been for the generosity of the Saints, who raised enough
money to help pay for their passage. When they arrived at the
wharf to leave the islands they were greeted by hundreds of
Saints who had gathered to bid them farewell. These Saints had
prepared a huge feast in their honor and planned a two-day
farewell meeting. Not only had the Saints gathered, but there
were also many non-members, government officials and others
who had known and learned to love Elder Cannon.

As was typical of his humility, he recognized his fame without taking credit for it. He knew the source and purpose of it:

> During my travels on the different islands I have been surprised at
> my own notoriety. They seemed to be as well acquainted with me

on Kauai as far as my name (Geogi Pukuniahi) and my proceedings were concerned, as they were on Maui. As far as a name is concerned I have got one on these lands, and the Lord has blessed me with influence far beyond what I ever could have expected, but I do not want the praise of men. I desire to be approved by my Heavenly Father and all the influence I can attain to over the hearts of the children of men I desire to have wisdom and grace to use it in spreading and building the kingdom of God.[101]

That night Elder Cannon recorded his feelings as he sat before the table laden with the sumptuous feast these people of modest means had prepared in his honor: "I could not eat, all my appetite had left me; the thoughts of leaving those with whom I had been associated in all circumstances for years on the closest terms of brotherly intimacy, deprived me of all relish for food; my feelings were poignant, and the pangs of parting deprived me of all feelings of joy at the prospect that was opening before me of seeing my mountain home with all its loved associations."[102]

As the ship bearing the elders set sail for San Francisco, Elder Cannon watched the islands fade into the distance. Only a few years before, the message of the Restoration had not been heard on these islands, and now there were "upwards of four thousand members of the Church in Hawaii."[103] He could not help but compare the difference between their modest arrival and this glorious send-off:

How great the contrast between our landing and our departure! We had landed there friendless and unknown—so far as man was concerned. Now there were thousands who loved us, who rejoiced in the truth of the gospel and in the testimony of Jesus. On that wharf that day was an illustration of the wonderful power of the gospel in creating love in the hearts of the children of men. We had gone forth weeping and bearing precious seed. The Lord had given us souls for our hire.[104]

Ship in harbor at Honolulu, Hawaii, ca. 1860

CHAPTER 5

The Western Standard Mission

Homecoming to the Valley

Sometime near the middle of August 1854, Elder Cannon and three of the other original missionaries to Hawaii sailed into San Francisco Bay. Elder Parley P. Pratt, then presiding over the Pacific Mission and living in San Francisco, was writing his autobiography. Pleased to see the young man whom he had known as a child in England and as a boy in Nauvoo, and with whose skills in publishing and penmanship he was

The Western Standard staff (from bottom left to right: Matthew F. Wilkie, George Q. Cannon, Joseph Bull, William H. Shearman, David H. Cannon).

acquainted, Brother Pratt prevailed upon Elder Cannon to assist him "some forty days in copying my autobiography."[1] Although it meant another six weeks away from home, Elder Cannon stayed to give the requested assistance. The time spent with Elder Pratt had far-reaching consequences later when George was again called to use his skills to help in Church publishing ventures. Near the first of October, having completed his forty-day service to Parley P. Pratt, Elder Cannon traveled south to San Bernardino, where in company with his friend, Elder Charles C. Rich the Apostle, he at last set out for home.[2]

The Journal History of the Church for November 28, 1854, noted his homecoming with one short line: "George Q. Cannon arrived in Salt Lake City, returning from his mission to the Sandwich Islands."[3] After a warm reunion with the Taylors and his brothers and sisters, three of whom he had not seen since leaving Winter Quarters in the summer of 1847, George gave his full attention to his intended, Elizabeth, who had been faithful to him even though the one-year calling as a gold-digging missionary had stretched into a five-year absence. The young couple lost no time; on December 11, 1854, less than two weeks after their reunion, George and Elizabeth were married. Speaking of his financial condition, Elder Cannon recalled: "When I went on my first mission, I was engaged to a young lady. After a lengthy absence, I came back as poor as missionaries generally do, but I got married twelve days after my return. I tried to get employment, but up to the day of my marriage I had not obtained it."[4]

Because of his poverty, George did not even have proper clothing to be married in and was obliged to borrow an ill-fitting suit. Afterwards he always reflected with laughter on the scene he created.[5] The day following his wedding, he succeeded in securing work. He presented himself at a certain business establishment and asked, "Do you have any work?" The proprietor made the usual excuses about not having enough funds to pay him. George replied, "I didn't ask for money; I asked for work. I'm willing to work for nothing rather than be idle." The quality and consistency of George's performance made him invaluable to his employer and he was soon on the payroll with the rest of the laborers.[6]

Elder Cannon was at no time without a Church assignment; while still in the islands he had been notified of his call as one of the presidents of the Thirtieth Quorum of Seventy, and shortly after his arrival home he was set apart to that office. In the early spring of 1855 the elders on the Sandwich Islands who had been involved with George Q. Cannon in ordering the printing press for the publication of the Book of Mormon wrote President Young requesting that Elder Cannon return to the islands to publish the book. Elder Cannon said, "I received an intimation from President Brigham Young that I would be called at the ensuing conference [April, 1855] to return on a mission to the Sandwich Islands."[7] Before the conference convened, however, Elder Pratt had reached the conclusion, in correspondence with the presidency of the mission on the Hawaiian Islands, that the press would be better located in San Francisco, as he had plans to use it there to publish a weekly newspaper for the Church. Brother Pratt also wrote Brigham Young requesting that Elder Cannon be sent to San Francisco to assist him.

During the six weeks that Elder Cannon had helped Brother Pratt with his autobiography, the Apostle had perceived that the young man possessed a journalistic talent that would be a great asset to the Apostle in publishing the periodical he proposed. When President Young learned that the press had been forwarded to San Francisco and when he received Brother Pratt's request for George's assistance, he called Elder Cannon on a mission to California—his third mission for the Church. The purpose of this mission was "to publish the Book of Mormon in the Hawaiian language and to assist Elder Parley P. Pratt in the publication of a paper."[8] President Young also called Elder Orson Hyde, who was at that time in charge of the Mormon settlement at Carson Valley, Nevada, to assist Elders Pratt and Cannon in the two proposed endeavors. In addition to this staff, President Young commissioned Elder Cannon to choose two other missionaries to assist him in typesetting and printing the Book of Mormon.

The Second Mission to California

On May 10, 1855, George Q. Cannon and his young wife set out for California, along with Joseph Bull and Matthew F. Wilkie, the two assistants he had chosen, and Elder Charles C. Rich, with whom he was making this journey for the third time. The *Deseret News* reported:

> Departure—on the 10th instant, General Charles C. Rich, one of the Twelve, started on his return to San Bernardino, accompanied by Elders George Q. Cannon, Joseph Bull, and Matthew F. Wilkie. Elders Cannon, Bull, and Wilkie will proceed to San Francisco to assist Elders Parley P. Pratt and Orson Hyde in establishing a printing office in that city for the purpose of publishing the Book of Mormon in the Hawaiian language, a newspaper, and such other publications as the cause of truth may require.

Elder Cannon translated the Book of Mormon into Hawaiian, while on his mission to the Sandwich Islands, and will attend to the proof-reading of that work, and be the foreman in the new office.

With such an array of ability, judgment, and skill, the establishment on the Pacific coast will be of vast utility in disseminating correct principles.[9]

Elder Cannon noted that the Lord had prospered him greatly during his five-month tenure in the valley and provided him the means for further service: "I had only been home five months when I went on another mission: and though it was in the winter time, I made means so fast that when I started on this mission, having been called to take my wife with me, I left Salt Lake City with a very excellent outfit—mules and wagon, provisions, etc."[10]

One of these mules caused some concern when the party reached southern Utah; she seemed to have strained herself pulling up some steep hills and could scarcely walk, let alone pull the wagon. Elder Cannon wrote in his journal for Monday, May 21, 1855: "I prayed over her and on her, twice, for if she failed, being the best animal in the team, I did not know scarcely how we would get along." For May 22, two entries mentioned her: "The Mule is somewhat better this morning," and "My mule had improved much."[11] The Lord was still blessing Elder Cannon as he always had in making possible the fulfillment of his missions.

The journey was mainly uneventful, as Joseph Bull indicated: "We had a pleasant trip across the plains, though somewhat warm while crossing the desert; but we got along first rate, and got our animals all through safe. We arrived at San Bernardino on the fourth of June, and found all well."[12] Elder Rich left them at San Bernardino, where he and Brother Amasa M. Lyman were presiding over a large settlement of Saints. When the Cannons and their two companions reached San Diego they secured passage on a steamer, arriving in San Francisco in the latter part of June.

Elder Cannon was greatly surprised and disappointed to discover that Parley P. Pratt had given up the idea of publishing the paper, had stored the press, and had departed for Utah a few days before their arrival. In March of that year, Brother Pratt had issued a prospectus for his periodical, the *Mormon Herald,* but having received "scarcely any encouragement, and not being aware of the arrangements made at April Conference to strengthen him, he had made up his mind, as he had been sometime absent from home, to return there."[13] Elder Cannon, learning Elder Pratt's travel route, set out immediately to overtake him. He caught up with him and learned the particulars of the publishing venture and of conditions in the Pacific Mission. "Finding that I had been called to labor under his direction, he deemed it wise, as he was leaving, to set me apart to preside over the Pacific Mission, subject to the direction of any of the Twelve Apostles who might visit or be called to labor in that part."[14]

Not long after this the three Apostles in that region, Charles C. Rich, Amasa Lyman, and Orson Hyde (who did not help in the printing operation as originally planned) confirmed Elder Cannon's appointment as mission president.[15] The area of the Pacific Mission was staggering in its dimensions; it included "northern California, Oregon and Washington territories, and the British and Russian and American possessions in the North."[16] Apparently, when Elder Cannon was being set apart as the mission president, Elder Pratt predicted that twenty-seven-year-old George Q. Cannon would be called to fill the vacancy in the Council of the Twelve that would be created at Elder Pratt's passing. Elder Cannon, and probably Elder Pratt as well, thought that the fulfillment of this prophecy would come many years in the future, since Brother Pratt was at that time only forty-eight years of age.[17]

Ka Buke A Moramona

Returning to San Francisco, Elders Cannon, Bull, and Wilkie rented an office on one of the major streets of the city and moved the press there from where Elder Pratt had stored it. In the trip from New York City around Cape Horn the ribs of the press had been broken; the Elders had them recast before they could commence printing the Book of Mormon. Elder Cannon, being the only one of the group who could understand Hawaiian, read the proofs as Elders Bull and Wilkie brought them from the press. Elder Cannon had Elizabeth read the Book of Mormon aloud to him in English while he followed along in Hawaiian, correcting the proofs as necessary.

One bothersome problem the printers experienced during the first few weeks of labor was the shortage of k's, which are numerous in the Hawaiian language. Reporting to President Young his progress on the Book of Mormon, Elder Cannon wrote: "For the first month after we commenced operations we had to issue it in octavo form, on account of the scarcity of lower case k's, which abound as plentifully in the Hawaiian language as e's do in English—but which the founder failed to send according to order, merely sending the usual proportion for an English fount [sic.]."[18]

The work progressed, as Brother Wilkie recorded in a letter written near the end of July: "We have got the press going, and have now printed off the first 16 pages of the Book of Mormon in the Hawaiian language. It looks well, and we feel highly gratified with our success so far. Elders Cannon, Bull, and myself are living together happy and free and rejoice in the spirit of the gospel."[19] Two months later the *Deseret News* quoted a letter from Elder Cannon further indicating their progress and their blessings from the Lord: "We now have out 240 pages of the Book of Mormon in the Hawaiian language and the prospect is good for the remainder being speedily done. I never in my life realized more visibly the hand of the Lord in aiding and assisting in every move that has been made; when the prospects, naturally speaking, were dark, and the way seemed to be almost completely blocked up, He has caused a gleam of sunshine to cross our path and we have been able to push forward with renewed courage to the accomplishment of all incumbent upon us."[20]

After several months of hard work, Elder Cannon was able to make this gratifying announcement to President Brigham Young:

> The book is finished, and I hope to be able to send you the first bound copy this mail. I feel grateful to our Heavenly Father for His kindness in enabling us to finish it, and thus help fulfill His words, spoken by His servants who wrote the Book, "That it should go forth to every nation, kindred, tongue and people."[21]

Many words of praise were sounded at the completion of this work. The *Deseret News* reported: "The translation of this work was made by Bro. Cannon while on his mission in the Sandwich Islands; it has been prosecuted to completion in book form under his superintendence, backed by arduous personal labors. [It] is an enduring monument to his faithfulness, patience, diligence, and perseverance amid many difficulties and disadvantages.[22]

As soon as they could be bound, two thousand copies of the Book of Mormon (*Ka Buke A Moramona*) were shipped to the islands. Before they sent the book to Hawaii, Elder Cannon sent many copies of a printed letter to be distributed among Saints and non-members alike telling them about *Ka Buka A Moramona*. A resolution passed at the spring conference of the Church on the islands reads: "Moved, That we tender to Elder George Q. Cannon of San Francisco our sincere thanks for the printed letter . . . which he sent us for distribution among this people; it has been the means of doing much good in preparing them to receive the Book of Mormon; and we feel to uphold and sustain Elder Cannon and associates, Elders Bull and Wilkie, in their labors in printing and publishing the Hawaiian translation of the Book of Mormon, and in all their efforts in the cause of truth."[23]

Elder Cannon's heart must have swelled at the realization of a dream he had had as a young missionary, barely able to understand the Hawaiian tongue. Reminiscing on those early years, he wrote: "When the translation was commenced, the Saints were few in number and poor, and there was no earthly prospect then in view of it ever being published; the Lord has most singularly, however, opened the way, and it is ready to go forth to another nation—a nation of red men—in their own language, to tell unto them the causes of their fathers' fall and the covenants made for their restoration."[24]

Conditions in California

The Cannon household included Brothers Bull and Wilkie,

and also George's seventeen-year-old brother David, who sometime after their arrival in San Francisco had been called on a mission to assist with the publication of the Book of Mormon. But on Friday, June 29, 1856, the household became even larger. Elizabeth gave birth to a fine baby boy, to whom the father proudly gave his own name. The newcomer caused rejoicing in the household, and a few days after his birth his father held a feast in the baby's honor and gave him a blessing. During the six months spent publishing the Book of Mormon, there was little income for this household. Young David recalled that "many mornings George Q. left without eating and with nothing in the house for Elizabeth and the baby."[25] While they were in this destitute condition, a wealthy Hawaiian planter made a gift of $3,000 to help the work along. It is a tribute to Elder Cannon's faith and trust in the Lord that he did not use any of this money to relieve his difficult circumstances, but sent all of it to the First Presidency. Brigham Young told Elder Cannon later that by sending this sum of money at that time he had saved the Church from a serious financial crisis.[26]

A lack of finances was not the only distressing condition encountered in California. The rough character of many low-class people who had been attracted to California during the days of the gold rush was in sharp contrast to the uplifting nature of the Saints with whom the publishing missionaries had been privileged to associate. Elder Wilkie gazed with righteous indignation upon the abominations that surrounded them: "When we first left the peaceful vales of Deseret, our eyes saw strange sights, our ears heard uncouth sounds; yes, men with the image and forms of God would blaspheme His holy name—would blast and curse themselves in almost every sentence which they uttered. Our souls shrunk back within us, and we would have wept for fallen humanity. We thought it would be more than we could then endure to live in such a place among such people."[27]

One of the products of the uncouth element in San Francisco was an unbridled lawlessness on all sides. "The spirit of murder and bloodshed rides rampant through the length and breadth of this country," Elder Cannon wrote to President Young. "And life is taken at the slightest provocation."[28] Regularly constituted forms of law enforcement were ineffective in curbing the flagrant disregard for law and order. In another letter to President Young, Elder Cannon portrayed the drastic means adopted to stifle this fierce crime wave:

> California is a hard country. As you will see by the accompanying papers which I send you, there had been a recurrence in San Francisco of the terrible scenes for which California has been so noted. A committee, styling themselves the Vigilance Committee, which is composed of twenty-nine men, whose acts are entirely secret and unknown, and whose word is law, hold the supreme power here at present. They have taken the law into their own hands and are determined that it shall be magnified; so far, the majority applaud and uphold their course, as they have acted with circumspection and order in the execution of their plans. But how terrible a situation for a people to be in, and how replete with evil and danger.[29]

But the missionaries were not despondent. Their dedication to the cause and the challenge of their work gave them little time to be downcast. As Elder Wilkie said, "We became some little reconciled to our situation after getting thoroughly at work."[30] Brother Cannon felt that whatever offenses they had to endure from the people were compensated by the assurance that they were engaged in the work of the Lord: "We all feel in good spirits being contented and happy, and can realize that, whether in the valleys of the mountains, on the islands of the sea, or in California, as long as we are in the line of our duty we can enjoy the spirit of peace and happiness."[31]

In Defense of Mormonism

President Young had Elder Cannon go to California for two reasons: first, to publish the Book of Mormon in Hawaiian; and second, to publish a newspaper in the defense of Mormonism. "While publishing this work [the Book of Mormon] . . . I maintained a constant correspondence with President Brigham Young. He still favored the publication of a newspaper, and appointed me to be its editor, and, by his kind, fatherly and hopeful counsels, gave myself and the Elders laboring with me continual encouragement in our labors."[32]

At a special conference of the Church, held in Salt Lake City on August 28 and 29, 1852, while George was still a missionary in Hawaii, the leaders of the Church made an official announcement of the doctrine and practice of plural marriage. This proclamation opened the floodgates of anti-Mormon slander: "From the islands of the sea; from Denmark, Sweden and Norway; from distant India as well as from England and the United States came reports of opposition and of increased persecutions ostensibly justified because of the Church's announced belief in the doctrine and practice of plural marriage.[33]

To combat this onslaught, which was carried on principally in the newspapers, the Church leaders initiated the publication of four weekly newspapers. The first of these, *The Seer*, was established in Washington, D.C., under the editorship of Elder Orson Pratt, and was issued from January 1853 until July 1855. Erastus Snow, also an Apostle, took charge of publishing *The St. Louis Luminary*, and issued it from November 1854 until December 1855. The third paper, published in New York City, was called *The Mormon*. Its editor, the former tutor of George Q. Cannon, his Uncle John Taylor, published this paper from February 1855 until September 1857. The same reason for which these three papers were published gave birth to the idea of having such a voice on the West Coast.

Along with the leaders of the Church, Brother Cannon saw the great need for a Church-oriented newspaper in California: "We have long needed a press; our enemies have had the privilege for years, of giving publicity to doctrines and views of our Church; they have maligned, vilified and misrepresented us; and the good which has been occasionally subscribed to us, they have taken particular pains to withhold from the world."[34]

Along the same line Elder Cannon wrote to his uncle, who had just begun publishing *The Mormon* in New York: "I feel anxious to see the paper published, as we need an organ on this western coast in which false impressions can be corrected and the knowledge of our principles spread more effectively."[35] Some of the false impressions Brother Cannon referred to were the fault of some so-called Mormons in that locality: "One of the things that has tended in no small degree to lessen 'Mormonism' has been the conduct of some who pass as Mormons, and when they get into any mean, nasty scrape, . . . the name of Mormonism is dragged in."[36] Brother Cannon told of encouragement, counsel, and even a suggestion for the name of the paper from Elder Orson Hyde: "I received a letter from Br. Orson Hyde in which he leaves me at liberty to publish and suggests 'The Western Standard' as the name or title; he also gives me good counsel in relation to the style of its matter, etc."[37]

Publication of the *Western Standard*

As soon as the Book of Mormon in Hawaiian had been completed, Elder Cannon turned his full attention to the establishment of this newspaper, which he did name the *Western Standard*. Although Elder Cannon was not one to flinch in the face of opposition, conditions were far from favorable: "Prospects in San Francisco for the establishment of a . . . newspaper, I found to be of a most discouraging character."[38] The lawless residents in San Francisco, some of whom held high offices in the corrupt city government, were not very tolerant of newspapers directed at their reformation. James King, editor of *The Bulletin*, a newspaper that openly criticized "the corrupt rule of the city and the abuses that were carried on under legal forms," was murdered in cold blood.[39] But Elder Cannon fearlessly determined to publish the *Western Standard* in spite of this violent climate. On January 4, 1856, the prospectus of the new Mormon paper was issued from the printing office, stating its purpose:

> It is the intention of the Subscriber to commence the publication of a Weekly Newspaper bearing the above title, the first number to be issued about the middle of February next, to be devoted to the interest of the Church of Jesus Christ of Latter-day Saints, to be an exponent of its doctrines, and a medium through which the public can derive correct information in relation to its objects and progress. Its columns will also contain items of general intelligence and the current news of the day, both foreign and domestic, which from our position, situated in the Queen City of the Pacific, we will be able to obtain at the earliest dates and in ample detail.[40]

Contrary to what might be expected, the members of the

Church themselves presented some opposition to the proposed publication. Members in the area numbered few because most who had joined the Church had either gathered to the Great Salt Lake Valley or to the Church settlement at San Bernardino. Elder Cannon commented, "The few who were left, and with whom I was brought in contact, seemed to have no faith that such an enterprise, as the publication of a newspaper advocating our doctrines, could be successfully carried out."[41] One of the reasons for the coldness and lack of support among members of the branch was that a short time before, they had been requested "under legitimate counsel" (Church leaders) to invest their money in a "vessel designed to sail between San Francisco and the Sandwich Islands for commercial purposes and also for the emigration from the islands to Utah of the native Saints." But "before anything was accomplished with the vessel it was wrecked and proved a total loss."[42] Having seen one Church-related project fail, they were skeptical, unwilling to contribute to another—especially one with as little promise as a Mormon newspaper in San Francisco. One of the leading brethren in San Francisco, recognizing Elder Cannon's need for capital but perhaps unwilling to supply funds himself, told Elder Cannon that a thousand dollars might be sufficient for him to accomplish the labors assigned. Elder Cannon replied, "I told him I had not a thousand dollars; but yet, with the help of God, they would be accomplished."[43] To justify his faith, the young editor reminded the branch members of the words of Nephi: "For I know that the Lord giveth no commandment unto the children of men, save he shall prepare a way for them that they may accomplish the thing which he commandeth them" (I Nephi 3:7).

Elder Cannon recorded another disappointing encounter he had with the local "Saints": "I having opened an office and commenced the publication of the book, the officers of the branch and conference asked me if I would not attend a meeting that they were going to hold. I supposed that they, seeing how destitute we were (myself and the two Elders who were with me, and my wife), were going to do something to assist us; but instead of that, they notified me that they would not be responsible for any debt of my contracting. They saw I was going ahead, but they did not want me to deceive myself with the idea that I could fall back on them and expect them to pay any debts that I might contract."[44]

This unmerciful statement of faithlessness aroused Elder Cannon's placid temperament to a state of holy anger:

> You can imagine what effect that would have on any of you. It stirred me up a good deal, and I prophesied to them—for I had the spirit of prophecy—and told them to get out of my way and not impede my work. They told me to shut up the office. I said to them, "I am sent here to do a work, and with God's help I will do it; and if you do not want to help in this, the Lord will raise up others that will."[45]

Elder Cannon later bore testimony to the fulfillment of this prophecy: "The Lord opened our way in a most signal manner. . . . . It really seemed to me that money grew in our hands, and . . . would go further and accomplish more, than four times the amount would under ordinary circumstances. . . . Friends were raised up on every hand, and though our pathway was not free from obstacles, yet the work moved off so successfully that we felt greatly favored and blessed of the Lord."[46]

Many of the friends who "were raised up" offered to loan Elder Cannon large sums of money for his publishing enterprise, but because he did not know how soon he would be able to repay them, he felt obligated to refuse their assistance: "Money was offered me by the thousands to assist me in my work. I did not avail myself of the offer because I knew if I did I would not be able to return it for a while."[47] President Brigham Young was so impressed with Elder Cannon's remarkable faith and business acumen that he used him as an example to others: "We sent Brother George Q. Cannon, one of Brother Taylor's nephews, to California, over a year ago last spring, to print the Book of Mormon in the Hawaiian language. He has printed a large and handsome edition of that book; has published a weekly paper and paid for it; has paid for the press and the type, and paid his board and clothing bills, though he had not a farthing to start with, that is, he went without purse and scrip."[48]

The short but energetic life of the *Western Standard* began Saturday, February 23, 1856, less than a month after the completion of the Hawaiian Book of Mormon. In the first issue Elder Cannon declared the purpose of the paper: "It is to correct [ill feelings], to make our principles and belief more publicly known, to give greater facilities for investigation, and to defend an innocent, much abused and injured people against the aspersions of their enemies that this paper has been started."[49] In the same issue Brother Cannon wrote a letter to the Saints of the Pacific Mission, calling for their support of this missionary venture and expressing his faith in the inspiration of those who had initiated it: "I am aware that it is an undertaking of no small magnitude, more especially at the present time in this country, to support the expense of the publication of a paper; but I have all confidence in the cause we have espoused and advocate, and, therefore, I do not have any fear on the subject. If I needed any assurance as to the propriety of such a move, the knowledge (which I have) that it is wisdom and counsel, would be sufficient, and would dispel every lingering doubt and inspire me to proceed."[50]

When the *Western Standard* first reached Great Salt Lake City, the *Deseret News* gave it this greeting: "A Star in the West began, on Saturday, the 23rd of Feb., 1856, to illume the horizon on the borders of our Pacific coast, for on that day and date Elder Geo. Q. Cannon issued No. I of Volume I of the "Western Standard," and clearly, steadily, and broadly may its genial rays lighten the lovers of truth in the pathway of righteousness."[51]

Format and Content of the Newspaper

The *Western Standard* was striking in appearance—its ornate masthead picturing the gathering of people from all nations to the tops of the mountains. On the mountains is a picture of a beautiful temple with the words "Gathering of the Nations" in the foreground. Spanning the entire page in bold type is the epithet "To Correct Mis-Representation We Adopt Self-Representation." Like its three sister papers, the *Standard* was a weekly publication that borrowed much of its material from the *Deseret News*. Its twenty-four columns covered the front and back of two pages. Subscriptions cost $5.00 per year "paid in advance." Many issues of the paper contained a list of sixty cities, mostly in California and Utah, but some as far away as Honolulu, Philadelphia, New York and Liverpool, and the name of a prominent Church member in each city who "will please act as agents for the *Western Standard*." The only engravings in the *Standard* appeared occasionally in its advertisements. The appearance and quality of the paper drew compliments even from a competitor. The *Sacramento State Journal* observed, "We have received a copy of the new Mormon weekly paper, published at San Francisco. In beauty of typographical appearance, it is unsurpassed by any other weekly paper in the state, and it is, apparently, edited with considerable ability."[52]

Although the contents of the *Western Standard* were centered chiefly around the defense of Mormonism, many other features were designed to attract non-Mormon readers. Most of these nonreligious articles were borrowed from various magazines and journals. Interesting subjects were treated such as "The Necessity of Sleep," "The Condensed History of Steam," "Is the Center of the Earth a Mass of Fire?" "How Ships Are Named," "Balloon Traveling," "The Wonders of the Microscope," and "Statistics of Chinese Population." Other articles dealt with practical helps for the readers: "The Value of Regularity in Feeding Cattle," "How to Look at the Eclipse," and "A Recipe for Nosebleeds." In keeping with its calling as a newspaper, many columns contained items of local, regional, national, and international news. Headlines for some of these columns read: "Indian Hostilities in Oregon Territory," "Alarming Increase in Highwaymen," "Late, Late, Late News from Europe," and "The Testimony of Earthquakes Felt in California." Some columns appeared weekly, such as "City Items," "News from the Interior" (meaning California), "News of Utah," and "Letters from the Elders."

Several serials contained the writings of prominent Latter-day Saints. The longest of these was a series of letters written by Orson Spencer, A. B., in reply to the challenges of a minister, Reverend William Crowel, A. M. Another item designed to be of service to the readers was a full-column listing of current prices in San Francisco, "corrected weekly," including everything from food to lumber, from clothing to medicine, and even tobacco. The minutes of general and regional conferences appeared frequently in the paper, as well as letters from the mission president to his elders and to the Saints in the field. Each issue contained an invitation to the public to attend the meetings held by the San Francisco branch. One weekly feature that attempted to give the readers a taste of culture was a space reserved at the top of column one for a few lines of poetry from both Mormon and non-Mormon pens. There was also an opportunity for readers to air their views in the space provided for letters to the editor.

The editor managed to secure a few paid advertisements to help defray the cost of the paper. In almost every issue a notice appeared proclaiming the virtues of "John Baptist's Trusses, Corsets, etc." Unhappy relatives from the East ran ads in the paper in an attempt to locate sons, husbands, and fathers who had been lost in the gold rush to California. Space that could not be filled with more profitable reading matter was devoted to "filler"—little anecdotes, sayings, and humor. Even this material was chosen to benefit the reader in some way. One thought-provoking aphorism asked: "Drinking water neither makes a man sick, nor runs him in debt, nor makes his wife a widow. Can as much be said of ardent spirits?" In a more humorous vein, this quip appeared on the same subject: "A coroner's jury ruled that the death of an inebriated man was 'Death by Hanging—round the rum shop.'"

Lifting a Voice of Warning and Disabusing the Public Mind

Meeting the publishing deadline each Saturday kept the four men so busy that Elder Cannon called one of his missionaries, William H. Shearman, from proselytizing activities to join the *Standard* staff. In a letter to President Young, editor Cannon wrote, "Since the paper started we have been kept very busy and have had but little time to spare. . . . The brethren set it up and Brother Wilkie works it off, while I keep myself busily employed writing, selecting, devil-ing, putting up and folding papers, etc."[53] Years later, in recalling the pressures of meeting these deadlines, Elder Cannon said of his editorials, "The first portion of nearly all of them was in type before the latter portion was written."[54]

Somehow, almost miraculously, the paper appeared every week except one: "We were compelled to suspend the publication of last week's paper in consequence of the severe illness of our little boy. He was seized, last Sunday, with violent spasms; I scarcely left his bed for five minutes for a week."[55] Although there was much faith and prayer in little George's behalf, the *Western Standard* for Saturday, November 15, 1856, carried this sad announcement: "George Q. Cannon, son of George Q. Cannon and Elizabeth Hoagland Cannon, died at the family home in San Francisco, California, age 4 months and 16 days."[56] The grief-stricken mother of the baby, knowing that her stay in San Francisco was only temporary, would not permit the child to be buried there, but had his body sealed in a metal casket, which they later carried back to the peaceful valley of Deseret to be laid near where Elizabeth herself wanted to be interred.[57] At the time of little George's death Elizabeth was expecting another child, who was born five months later and named John Quayle Cannon.

In December 1856 Elder Cannon had a spiritual experience in connection with the death of Jedediah M. Grant, a member of the First Presidency of the Church. Although Elder Cannon was far away in California and knew nothing of President Grant's death, an unusual feeling of unrest came over him on the day the

Church leader died. He related this experience in a letter to Brigham Young: "I had a singular feeling come over me while one of the brethren was opening the meeting by prayer. My mind was caught away and I saw our paper (the *Standard*) in mourning, and it was made known to me that it was for one of the First Presidency. The thought of such an event was so disagreeable to me that I endeavored to drive it away, and felt to condemn myself for allowing my mind to permit such a phantasy (as I tried to persuade myself it was) to enter my brain; but I could not get rid of the feeling, nor of an indefinable feeling of sadness which I had afterwards, and which I alluded to in my remarks to the people."[58]

Although Elder Cannon's publishing duties occupied most of his time, his responsibilities as mission president were not neglected. Apparently there was little proselytizing activity in the mission when he arrived. Most of the members had migrated; and those who remained were scattered. A few weeks after his arrival in San Francisco he wrote to Brigham Young requesting that elders be sent to the San Francisco area to teach the gospel to those he hoped to reach through the influence of the paper: "I have thought that I would take the liberty of suggesting to you the propriety of sending some Elders to this country to labor in preaching etc., that if perchance a spirit of inquiry might be aroused through the instrumentality of the press, there would be somebody on hand to take advantage of it, and lay our principles more fully before them."[59]

Another portion of this same letter expressed his feelings about the lack of success of the elders in California and his desires to change this trend in his mission: "I am aware that the prospect is not very flattering, especially when the success of the Elders of San Bernardino is remembered; but the want of success that seemed to attend their efforts may to some extent, in my opinion, be attributed to the want of energy on their part. I do think, however, that if some good men could be selected who would—as remarked by Bro. Jedediah to me at Parowan while speaking of the success of Elders—'hang like a puppy to a root,' much good might be done, and many be gathered out of California to swell the number of those who are ranging themselves under the banner of the Lamb."[60] These same feelings concerning a need for improvement in missionary labors were echoed in a letter to the elders in his mission, which he sent them through the pages of the *Western Standard:* "It is time, brethren, you should arouse yourselves from the lethargy into which many have fallen, and awake to the importance in being diligent in the work of the Lord. The work, which many of you received with so much joy, has not lost any of its original potency or virtue."[61]

Elder Cannon was also interested in the welfare of the Church members in his mission, most of whom were widely spread and not associated with any organized branch of the Church. In the first issue of the *Western Standard* he requested that all those who wished to continue as members of the Church write to him of their numbers and locations so he could send elders to organize them into branches.[62] Because many people were preoccupied with the worldly wealth of the gold rush, the elders spent most of their time warning the people and found relatively few converts. The *Western Standard* was a far-reaching voice in this warning. The fourteenth General Epistle of the Church, December 1856, contained this reference to the *Western Standard:* "In California, the *Western Standard* is faithfully warning the people, under the able care and guidance of Br. George Q. Cannon. . . . The publication of that paper has proved very useful and beneficial in correcting public opinion, and in exercising a salutary influence over the few to be found in that land who are seekers after truth. Gold is the shrine at which they bow, and the truth emanating from High Heaven's King has but few admirers."[63]

Much of the public disfavor of Mormonism could be attributed to the numerous unfavorable newspaper articles and editorials that many presses, large and small, published frequently. Elder Cannon was overwhelmed at the amount of publicity the Mormons had in the United States, considering that there were only 100,000 of them in a nation of 26 million people. He wrote:

> Who are the "Mormons," and what are their pretensions and numbers, that there should be such a continual excitement maintained relative to them and their movements? To read all that is published about them, and witness the interest which is manifested in all their doings, it might be supposed that they are one of the most numerous and formidable people on the face of the earth. . . . An exploring expedition, a military company, or a colony cannot be organized by the "Mormons,"—a review cannot be held—President Brigham Young cannot leave Great Salt Lake City on a pleasure excursion, without every such item being chronicled and commented upon by the press from one end of the land to the other.[64]

The public appetite for sensational stories about the strange polygamous Mormons provided an insatiable market for the deluge of articles. Because readers did not seem to demand that these stories be true, editors took no pains to ensure their veracity. In fact, Elder Cannon observed that they seemed to prefer falsehood: "It is astonishing how easily they are sold on everything pertaining to us, as a people; they greedily swallow up the most absurd lies, and prefer them, all the time, to plain, straight-forward, reasonable truth."[65] He reported one such lie to President Brigham Young: "The latest lie in circulation here is one concerning your arrest on a charge of treason by Col. Sumner, with 80 dragoons, and his departure with you in custody for Washington 'unmolested by the Mormons.' This happened on the 25th of June, and as you did not seem to be aware of it on the 4th of July, the date of your letter, I send you the news."[66]

The *Western Standard* lost no time in making its presence known. Its fearless young editor did not hesitate to issue stern rebukes and brilliant counterattacks against the offending papers. The *Sacramento State Journal*, the same paper that earlier had complimented the *Western Standard*, succumbed later to the public taste for Mormon scandal, and thereby earned this scathing editorial comment: "The *Sacramento State Journal* has of late taken particular pains to publish every low, scurrilous article that could be found about the Mormons. Not content with republishing everything of this kind that could be selected, the editors have been to the pains to manufacture items to suit, thinking it no disgrace to utter barefaced lies to make a good story. The unenviable notoriety which this paper has recently gained throughout the state for being the most mendacious and corrupt sheet published within its limits, makes its slanders on Mormonism and the Mormons comparatively innocuous."[67]

An example of the "barefaced lies" the *Western Standard* decried appeared in a newspaper called the *Golden Era*. The editor presented an "exposé" of the "tricks resorted to by Joseph Smith in the working of miracles—in resurrecting the dead by burying live men in coffins, with tubes through the earth for supplying the subject with air; in walking on the water by ingeniously arranging a plank platform two inches below the surface;

in the finding of the Book of Mormon,—the coinage of a poetical lunatic, with its alterations and elaborations by the prophet."[68]

Elder Cannon refuted such accusations of fraud by pointing out the parallelism between them and those that surrounded the miracles in the life of Christ. The Pharisees accused the Apostles of effecting a "resurrection" by stealing into the tomb at night and carrying away the body of the Savior, and then announcing to the world that he had risen from the dead. Elder Cannon pointed out that the readers would not place any credence in such a story, and neither should they take stock in what the *Golden Era* had "trumped up" about the Prophet Joseph. It was with reasoning such as this and with boldly persuasive rhetoric that the editor of the *Western Standard* met his foes.

By far the most forceful writing in the *Western Standard* were the defenses of Mormonism that Elder Cannon made in his editorials. The defense of polygamy dominated those editorials, this doctrine being the most controversial. One editorial on the subject with which Elder Cannon took issue was printed in the *Daily Sun*, whose editor supported the idea that a railroad from California to Utah would have the effect of breaking up the Mormons' "abominable and infernal system of polygamy" and compel them "to restrain their depravities within due bounds." The railroad would provide the means whereby the enslaved women of Utah could escape to California, where men were plentiful and would be willing to marry them. To this Brother Cannon replied: "They do not know the women of Utah, or they would never imagine that they would descend so low as to take up with their offers. . . . The idea of such women being 'little better than bond slaves,' is simply ridiculous, and no public journalist, who is posted up in the affairs of Utah, . . . would advance it, unless it was with a design to misrepresent."[69]

Brother Cannon then reprinted a statement made by this same editor in another issue of the *Sun,* in which, attempting to make another point, he enumerated some of the sins of the California society: "Wives are being constantly swapped, and an almost interminable series of murders, robberies, arsons, rapes, seductions and other fashionable crimes are continually being perpetuated." Elder Cannon took full advantage of this tirade, attempting to hang the *Sun* editor with his own rope: "Not satisfied with having California a pandemonium, he must use his influence to innoculate the Mormon people with the Sodomic virus of California corruptions! . . . We can assure the gentleman . . . in behalf of the women of Utah, that they have not the slightest desire to partake of the liberty (?) they would offer them. They have witnessed the corruptions that abound in the world, and have joyfully made sacrifices to get to Utah, where virtue and chastity are respected. They would rather die in those mountains, than be forced to live amid the corruption and villainy that so plentifully abound in this country."[70]

Another editor who incurred a devastating rebuke from Elder Cannon, wrote in the *California American* about the monstrous evil of polygamy that the Mormon missionaries were teaching to the natives on the Sandwich Islands. He concluded his attack by suggesting that the elders "ought to be hung up like pirates." As part of the chastisement Elder Cannon delivered, he declared that men who held the same views as the editor of the *California American* "are unworthy of the society of their fellowman and should be shunned as enemies of their race. Had they lived in the days of Christ they would have been in the crowd who cried, 'Crucify him, crucify him!'" Brother Cannon further maintained that "if the Latter-day Saints are preaching 'a cursed doctrine' on the Sandwich Islands, they are preaching accursed doctrines in California; for we preach but one doctrine wherever we go." He inquired whether the editor would advocate hanging for those who propagated the doctrine in California. He then boldly asserted that he was the first individual to teach the principle of polygamy in the islands, and suggested that before the editor go to Hawaii to

> execute the sanguinary vengeance they have decreed against the "Mormons" they had better commence with [me], as I have not only been "guilty of propagating 'Mormonism'" there, but [am] also engaged in the same delightful occupation here, and, the Lord being [my] helper, intend to follow the business for the remainder of [my] life and throughout the endless ages of eternity.[71]

This repartee of Elder Cannon's was successful in securing at least a halfhearted retraction of the hanging sentence. In the next issue of the *California American*, its editor averred that he did not wish it understood that he literally favored publicly executing Mormon preachers, but had made this "exaggeration" in a "momentary burst of indignation." He then went on to another vile tirade against the Church in which he used extremely crude and abusive language and concluded by suggesting again that Mormons were common enemies to mankind and "ought to be hung up every one of them." The effect of the *Western Standard's* rebuke seemed to have worn off by the end of the new article. Elder Cannon, therefore, felt obliged to administer another one:

> Not being subject to "momentary bursts of indignation," nor being in the habit of dealing in "exaggerations," we confess that we cannot compete with the editor of the *American* in the use of low, abusive and ungentlemanly epithets. In this he excels us. His

past education and experience have given him such ready command of ribaldry that we must forever despair of being able to
emulate him. . . . But as the editor of the *American* is probably not
aware of the fact, that slang and abuse do not pass among sensible
and well bred people for argument and ability, we take the pains
to enlighten him, and to inform him, also, that his use of such
terms as *lying hypocrite—miserable fanatic—impostor—filthy monstros-
ity—foul superstition,* etc., only betrays a mean and ignoble spirit
that, by its proficiency in vulgarity, would endeavor to hide its
lack of sense.[72]

Elder Cannon's slashing rebuttals did not go unnoticed by
the California newspaper editors, and they began to restrain
themselves in what they wrote about the Church. The *Deseret
News* affirmed Elder Cannon's success: "The *Western Standard* is
causing reckless editors to be a little more shy in dishing up lies,
slander, misrepresentation, and vituperation concerning the
Mormons."[73] *Western Standard* subscribers throughout Utah
lauded not only Elder Cannon's defense of the truth but Brothers John Taylor's and Erastus Snow's as well. At a celebration in
honor of the fourth and twenty-fourth of July, 1857, held at
Nephi, Utah, the following amusing tribute was read in honor of
these three publishers: "Editors John Taylor, Erastus Snow and
George Q. Cannon—May the Snow storm blow, the Cannon
roar, and the Taylor cut until the gain-sayers of Zion are si-
lenced."[74]

Another victim of Editor Cannon's sharp pen was an apostate Mormon missionary by the name of William Hyde, who
was preaching against polygamy and the Church in the Sandwich
Islands, in San Francisco, and later in England. A San Francisco
newspaper, the *Pacific,* published parts of his lectures and praised
his gallant efforts in editorials, declaring that this modern David

would annihilate Mormonism, polygamy, and the "legion of a false prophet." The *Western Standard* did not have the same estimation of Mr. Hyde's potential. In reviewing Hyde's activities, Elder Cannon apologized: "Our readers will please pardon us for troubling them with so long a notice of a person so insignificant and trifling as this individual has proved himself to be. We really think him beneath our personal notice; but in our character of journalist and publisher of news, we could not well avoid noticing his lectures."[75]

Mr. Hyde's lectures, which Brother Cannon characterized as "stale slander," consisted of a rehearsal of the "tyranny and wrong, corruption and sorrow, vice and crime, contradictions and inconsistencies in doctrines, ridiculous pretensions miserably supported, outrageous imposture and intolerant bigotry," which Hyde supposedly witnessed with horror during his nine years of residence in Salt Lake City. Elder Cannon handled him thus:

> But, though fully aware, as we learn from his own acknowledgments, of the existence of this corruption, vice and degradation in "Mormonism"; with his eyes wide open to "the absurdities in its doctrines, the abominations in its practices, and its demoralizing influence over its votaries,"—he starts from Great Salt Lake City as a missionary to the Sandwich Islands; forsakes his wife and child—leaving them to the tender mercies of those whom he now terms thieves, villains, and murderers; journeys nine hundred miles in the character of a missionary of "Mormonism"; suffers himself to be published as such in the public prints, lectures as such in San Francisco—not only upon the other principles of "Mormonism," but even upon polygamy, which he now declares that he knew, for some time previous to leaving Utah, to have originated in the lusts of Joseph Smith.[76]

Elder Cannon found one of the articles that had been published while Mr. Hyde was a missionary for the Church lecturing in San Francisco on his way to the Sandwich Islands. Surprisingly enough, this article reporting the virtue and divinity of polygamy had been published in the same newspaper, the *Pacific*, which now supported his contradictions. Elder Cannon reprinted one statement about what Mr. Hyde said in his lecture, which proved him to be a liar. Elder Hyde said that "he had seen more obscenity, licentiousness and crime in this city [meaning San Francisco] in one night, than during the whole of his stay of several years in Utah."[77] Elder Cannon concluded his devastating exposé of Mr. Hyde with this statement: "He could afford to preach and disseminate these 'errors' for nothing—go without purse or scrip to do it; but now, when he wished to refute them, he must be paid half a dollar per head! What inconsistency!"[78]

The Mission Ends

On July 24, 1857, word reached the Salt Lake Valley that an army of 2,500 men had been ordered to march to Utah to put down a so-called insurrection there. President James Buchanan, alarmed by rumors and false reports concerning Mormon rebellion, decided to impose federally appointed officials upon the people of Utah under the protection of this army. The Latter-day Saints, who had become inured to mob violence parading under the guise of legitimate government authority, braced for war. In addition to military preparations, the Church leaders called home from their scattered outposts Apostles, missionaries, and Saints living in the most outlying settlements such as San Bernardino and Carson Valley, Nevada. When news of the "invasion" reached California, the anti-Mormon papers, feeling renewed by apparent government support of their outlandish opinions about the Mormons, intensified their attacks. In his editorials Elder Cannon faithfully represented the Latter-day Saints as a peace-loving people, but fearlessly declared their intentions to maintain their freedom. He wrote:

> If the collision be forced upon them—if the determination be to compel them to cease the practice of their religion, to deprive them of their rights and privileges as freemen, to make them slaves in fact—then we, were we in Utah, would say, Let it come; with God to defend the right, we will risk the consequences. We would say, Let the rugged defiles of the Rocky Mountains become a second Thermopylae, where the sons of illustrious sires will contend for the precious rights bought by the blood of their fathers and bequeathed to them as the most inestimable boon that they could bestow. We would say, that rather than part with our religion, we, with God's assistance, will part with life.[79]

When it became apparent that Elder Cannon's editorials actually reflected Brigham Young's determination to fight rather than surrender their freedom and safety, some non-Mormons felt great concern for the safety of the army: "It was strongly advocated in one or two of the leading journals that George Q. Cannon should be seized and held as hostage for the safety of the officers of the army."[80] Like most of the material published about Mormonism, this threat was idle talk. But under the circumstances Elder Cannon felt it wise to send Elizabeth and little John Q. back to Utah in the care of his brother David. These three traveled south to San Bernardino, where they joined a company of emigrants bound for the Valley. Because they left so late in the year, about the end of November, they ran into extremely cold weather, and little seven-month-old John's feet were frost-bitten. The party arrived in Salt Lake on New Year's Day.[81]

Elder Cannon valiantly continued to defend the truth by publishing the weekly *Standard* until he was directed to return to Utah. On December 1, 1857, Elders Orson Pratt and Ezra T. Benson, along with some other missionaries, arrived in San Francisco on their way home from England. Because of the excitement over Johnston's Army, they had traveled incognito. They counseled Elder Cannon to settle up his business quickly and depart with them for Great Salt Lake City. After making this strenuous journey again, he arrived at his home in the mountains on January 19, 1858.[82]

Upon leaving California at the closing of his third mission, Elder Cannon recorded these feelings in his journal: "I leave San Francisco without a sigh of regret; . . . I feel clear from the blood of this people; I have labored diligently, labored to lay before them the principles of salvation by means of the press and public preaching, but to all the offers of salvation they have turned a deaf ear, and they have treated all our testimonies and warning as idle tales."[83] In bidding farewell to readers of the *Western Standard*, both friend and foe, Elder Cannon answered with this powerful testimony the assertion of many that sending troops to Utah would mark the end of Mormonism:

> The editor of the Herald deceives himself and those who believe what he writes, when he says that "the days of Mormonism at Salt Lake are numbered." The cannon are not cast, the muskets or rifles not made, the powder and ball not manufactured, nor the men to use them either born or conceived, that will destroy "Mormonism." Mark our words, gentlemen, it will live, though all earth and hell array themselves against it.[84]

Masthead of The Western Standard

Title page of the Hawaiian Book of Mormon, translated and published by George Q. Cannon

CHAPTER 6

The Eastern States Mission

Troubled Times in Utah

WHEN GEORGE Q. CANNON arrived at the Great Salt Lake Valley on January 19, 1858, he was no doubt filled with varied emotions. He was returning to his loved mountain home in Zion after spending nearly two years in "Babylon." There were joyful reunions with friends, relatives, Church leaders, and most important with Elizabeth and his little son John. But the ominous forebodings of an impending clash between an army of the United States and the Saints must have blunted the joy of the

First Presidency and Quorum of the Twelve (George Q. Cannon is third from right)

occasion. The 2,500 troops under the command of Colonel Albert Sidney Johnston were wintered 113 miles east of Salt Lake City in the Green River country of Wyoming. Brigham Young's "scorched earth" harassment tactics had delayed their threatened entrance into the valley. Without firing a single shot, guerilla militia under the command of Robert T. Burton, Lot Smith, Porter Rockwell, and others had burned the foliage that the army had anticipated using to feed their livestock along the route. This militia had also burned supply trains and generally impeded the progress of the army until the winter snows had forced it to encamp short of its destination.[1]

Many people feared that spring would bring a bloody confrontation between the Mormons and the soldiers. A message from General Daniel H. Wells, commander of the Nauvoo Legion, the militia that was preparing to protect the valley, recommended that all the Saints be united, "praying for one thing, and not being divided in their wishes and desires to God. We are all to pray that the soldiers might return, and that we might not have to shed their blood."[2] On the very night of Brother Cannon's arrival he was appointed adjunct general in the Nauvoo Legion, and soon he became very involved in preparing the defenses of the valley. In March, the prospects of troops forcing their way into the valley seemed so probable that President Young determined to vacate Salt Lake City and the northern communities, and even burn them if necessary. In the next several weeks 30,000 residents of northern Utah each packed up a few provisions and moved south into neighboring communities.

In early April, President Young called on George Q. Cannon to perform another publishing mission.[3] He was to remove the press and type and some supplies of the *Deseret News* to Fillmore, Utah, and publish the paper there, reducing it in size from eight to four pages. President Young apparently had plans to conceal the place of publication, because part of the press was taken to Parowan and part of it to Fillmore in order to make obscure its actual location. But if any issues of the paper were published at Parowan, the masthead did not show it, and it seems quite likely that the *News* never was actually printed there.[4] Fillmore was located on Chalk Creek, 150 miles south of Salt Lake; and because of its central location, in 1851 the legislature had selected it as the capital of Utah Territory. In 1853 construction began on an elaborate state house, and the legislative session of 1855–56 convened in the single wing of the building, which was all that was ever completed. The territorial capital was returned to Salt Lake City in 1856, leaving this stately structure vacant. It was from the basement of this building that Brother Cannon issued the *Deseret News* each week from April 15 to September 1, 1858.[5]

Editor Cannon defended the Mormon position with the same zeal in the *Deseret News* as he had in the *Western Standard*.[6] Many newspapers in the United States had become very critical of the president's overreactions to the Utah situation and lashed out at "Buchanan's blunder." Of course, Elder Cannon took great delight in republishing many of these sharp attacks on Buchanan. The August 18 edition of the *News* made reference to an Iowa newspaper's opinion of President Buchanan's judgment: "A murderer having escaped from jail at Webster, Iowa, the local paper suggested that a detective be sent to Kansas to apprehend him before Buchanan appoints him to an office."[7]

Having fun at the president's expense was not limited to non-Mormon writers. John Jaques penned this biting poem entitled "The Mormon Question":

There's been a great commotion
About the Mormon war;
It has, throughout the nation,
Set the wisest men ajar.
Some think we are rebellious,
Guilty of every crime;
Some think we're hardly dealt by;
And have been all the time.

A pack of graceless scoundrels,
Who've been unhung too long,
Said all things bad of Utah,
Said them with trumpet tongue.
And editors and parsons
Caught up the welcome strain
And made it through the country
Reverberate again.

Buchanan then was seeking
To get an honor'd name;
To win, while he was ruler,
A lasting wreath of fame.
The world said, "Strike the Mormons!"
Though we were not to blame.
He struck! and won confusion,
And everlasting shame.

The courtesy to send us
A word, he was without;
From hearsay and the papers
We guessed the matter out.

But he sent forth his army
To scare us! Didn't we quail!
And when he could not come it,
His heart began to fail . . .[8]

    A few days before Elder Cannon left Salt Lake City for Fillmore with the press, he visited President Young's office, where he first met Sarah Jane Jenne,[9] a beautiful eighteen-year-old girl "with sparkling grey-blue eyes and dark, luxuriant hair."[10] The girl's father had caught gold fever and had deserted his family. Her mother then married Elder Franklin D. Richards, the Apostle who was also married to her mother's sister, and he adopted the children, although they never took his name.[11] George "received an impression that amounted to knowledge that she [Sarah Jane] was to be his wife. She received the same manifestation."[12] The pressure of his most recent assignment to Fillmore did not allow time for a long courtship; in fact, with Elizabeth's consent they were married by President Brigham Young one week later, on Sunday, April 11, 1858. The trip to Fillmore with the press was the only semblance of a honeymoon that Sarah Jane had. And this trip was made in the company of Elizabeth, baby John Q., and George's brother, David Cannon.[13]

    In February 1858 Colonel Thomas L. Kane had arrived from Washington, D. C., via San Francisco. A devoted friend and confidant of the Mormons, he had by now secured the permission of President Buchanan to come to Utah and act as a liaison between President Young and Alfred Cumming, the new federally appointed governor of the Utah Territory, who was being escorted by the army. Colonel Kane arranged to have the new governor enter the valley unescorted by troops about the middle of April; and with the assistance of a special peace commission that

arrived in June a compromise settlement was worked out between the federal government and the Saints whereby the troops
were permitted to march through the deserted city. The army
was not allowed to stop in Great Salt Lake, where men were
standing by ready to put the torch to everything that would burn
if the terms of this agreement were not complied with. According to agreement, the army marched on to Cedar Valley, about
thirty miles to the south, where they established a military
camp.[14] With the protection of a presidential pardon for their
supposed rebellion, the Saints were free to return to their homes.
Elder Cannon published the following notice in the *Deseret News,*
July 14, 1858:

> RETURNING TO THEIR HOMES—The First Presidency
> left Provo at 6 p.m. of June 30th, and arrived at their homes in
> Great Salt Lake City at 3 a.m. of July 1st. All who wish to return
> are at liberty to do so.[15]

Mission Call to the Eastern States

Elder Cannon continued to publish the *News* until early September, when he was directed to return the press to Great Salt
Lake City. When he reached Payson with his heavily loaded wagons, a messenger from President Young met him with some un-
expected news. If he had any dreams of finally being able to
settle down to a "normal" life, those dreams would have to wait.
The message contained another mission call, this time to the
Eastern States. Elder Cannon recalled this incident in these
words:

> At Payson at noon on Monday, as I was unhitching my team
> at Brother William B. Preston's. . . . Brother John Bollwinkle drove

up with a carriage and mules and handed me a note. It was from President Young, and was dated the day previous, Sunday. He informed me that I had been appointed to go East on a mission. The company I was to go with expected to start the next day (the day I received the note), and he wished me to come to the city as quickly as I could. In reply to my inquiry, the messenger said he would be ready to start back as soon as he had eaten his dinner and fed his mules.

While he was gone, I gathered up what clothing and bedding and weapons I needed for the journey, and in about three quarters of an hour we were on our way to Salt Lake City, where we arrived the next morning as day was breaking.[16]

The conveyance that had been sent to carry Brother Cannon to the city had room enough for only one of his wives. Although both of them were expecting babies, Sarah Jane, who had just turned nineteen, insisted that George take Elizabeth and John Q. with him in the carriage. Leaving his young wife and heavy wagons containing the press equipment in the care of his brother David, he journeyed all night and reported to President Young early the next morning. Upon seeing him, Brigham Young turned to the others in the office and said, "Didn't I tell you it would be so? I knew I had but to call, and here he is!"[17] President Young's statement shows that George's great devotion and faithfulness had not gone unnoticed and that the prophet had come to respect and trust him.

Later that same day, Elder Cannon left for the East. He had great concern for his wives and son and the two babies who were expected to be born in January and March of the next year. Describing their homeless condition, he wrote: "As I had only been home from a mission, a few weeks before I went to Fillmore, and had been absent several years before on another mission, I had no home in Salt Lake City. In leaving my family at the roadside, therefore, I left them with no bright prospect for comfort and ease during my absence. But they uttered no complaints. They put their trust in the Lord and during the two years of my absence, He was their benefactor and friend."[18] An entry in his journal gives evidence of his great trust in the Lord and his devotion to Him in regard to the future of his family: "Before starting I prayed with and blessed Elizabeth and John Q., committing them and Sarah Jane and all that belonged to me into the hands of the Lord."[19]

The journey from Salt Lake to Florence, Nebraska, took more than five weeks and was comparatively uneventful until his company reached the Loup Fork of the Platte River, where Elder Cannon narrowly escaped death. After spending the better part of the day swimming and wading back and forth across the river in attempts to find a suitable place for the wagons to cross, he became extremely tired. The river bottom was full of heavy quicksand and was very fatiguing to wade in. When night came he found himself on the opposite side of the river from where the members of his party were. Rather than cause his companions to worry all night for his safety, he decided to swim the river once more to join them for the night. Because it was getting late, he determined to swim directly across the river rather than take the time to find the shallow but longer route. George was a good swimmer, but after plunging into the swift current he discovered that he was more fatigued than he had thought. This exhaustion, combined with the heavy, fearsome darkness of a moonless night, caused Elder Cannon to panic and fear for his life. Relating this incident later he wrote:

As I recall the scene now, I see the thick darkness which hides everything from view. I hear the rush of the stream as I battle desperately with it, and I feel the sinking of the heart at the thought of being lost in that strange place, with not one of my family or friends to ever know my fate. I thought of all my past life, the promises that had been made to me, the sweet hopes I had entertained for the future, the important mission that had been given me. And was this to be the close of my career? What a message to send to my fellow servants and my family—that I had disappeared, no one knew how or where, but presumably by drowning in the Loup Fork of the Platte River.[20]

Realizing that he was helpless to save himself, he cried to the Lord to rescue him, and once again his prayers were answered: "Can I make anyone understand the unspeakable joy I felt when I struck the bar and found myself in shallow water! I sank on my knees exhausted in the sand, inexpressibly thankful for my deliverance from death."[21]

In Defense of Mormonism

This mission to the East was semi-political. The country had been flooded with misrepresentations and falsehoods about Utah and the Church, rumors that had been the basis for sending the army to the Territory. "The whole affair had been ingeniously and artfully worked up by persons who were interested in creating hostility between the general government and the people of Utah."[22] Although Governor Cumming and the peace commission had furnished the president with the truth and had dispelled many baseless stories, this correct information had not been made available to the general public, who consequently nurtured many false and negative notions about the Mormons. Part of Elder Cannon's mission was to do all he could to enlighten the general public and win the favor of editors and men who had political influence in Washington. He was also given the responsibility to preside over the Eastern States Mission and to act as the Church emigration agent for the East.[23]

The genesis of Elder Cannon's mission to the East may have been President Brigham Young's reading of a correspondence from former President Millard Fillmore to the *New York Herald.* Brigham Young characterized the statements made in the letter as "almost clear 'Lye [sic.].'" The same day the "Journal History of the Church" recorded that "President Young talked of sending George Q. Cannon . . . to the States . . . to take some interest in getting pieces published in the dailies in the States."[24] Brother Cannon's fearless but diplomatic defense of the truth had impressed President Young, and he felt that some good could be accomplished by having this young missionary editor serve as an ambassador of the Church in influencing political and editorial opinion in the East. Another factor that undoubtedly contributed to President Young's decision to send Brother Cannon on this mission was the fact that Colonel Thomas L. Kane had a great deal of political influence in Washington and could acquaint Brother Cannon with the process of political maneuvering and introduce him to Kane's prominent friends.

While Colonel Kane was in Utah rendering his self-initiated and invaluable service as peacemaker between the Mormons and the federally dispatched officials and army, he had many interviews with President Young. During one of these conversations Kane mentioned that his health was not good and expressed some feeling that he might not live much longer. To this President Young replied, "Brother Thomas, the Lord sent you here, and he will not let you die. No! you cannot die until your work is done. I want to have your name live with the saints to all eternity. You have done a great work, and you will do a greater work still."25 A study of the efforts of Colonel Kane on behalf of the Mormons until his death in 1883, twenty-five years later, clearly indicates the fulfillment of this prophecy. Many of these efforts were made in connection with this diplomatic mission of Brother Cannon's. It is not surprising that one of the things Elder Cannon did soon after arriving in the East was to call on this beneficent gentleman.

In a letter from Philadelphia to President Young, Brother Cannon mentioned the kind of advice and hospitality Colonel Kane gave him: "Immediately upon my arrival here I waited upon Colonel Thomas Kane, delivered his trunk and sack which you sent, and handed him my letter of introduction. My reception by him was most cordial, and he spent the greater part of the day in hearing the news from the valley in which he was much interested, and in giving me a thorough insight into the condition of affairs here and the policy to be pursued. He told me the editors he wished me to see, and stretched the style of conversation and the points to be made with every one."26

Elder Cannon further reported that the colonel believed that there were only a few editors who had the rare gift of understanding the public mind and of knowing "how to manufacture public opinion on any question." The Colonel wanted him to meet these editors, feeling that "if they led off, others would readily follow." He advised President Cannon to assume a particular image in presenting himself to these editors:

In regard to my own story, I was to be a man of business, a "Mormon" of course, with some means at command, desirous of influencing public opinion and relieving myself and co-religionists from the weight of odium that had been so unjustly and cruelly

heaped upon us; had a little means which I was willing to devote
to accomplish this; but knowing the power of the press, and the
experience they had in its management and in the manufacture of
public opinion, had called upon them to ask their advice on the
subject; would well written articles as correspondence and editorial be likely to effect anything? What did they think of it? Being
experienced in these matters would they be kind enough to sug-
gest the course most likely to effect what I desired, etc.? There
were several unwritten chapters of the history of our troubles,
which, if made public, I felt assured would make a great change in
public opinion, etc., etc.[27]

After visiting with many of these editors, Elder Cannon reported to Colonel Kane, who then followed up by visiting them
himself, and Kane, "possessed of the results of my conversations
with them, was enabled to learn their true position and feelings
and shape things accordingly." As part of the image Kane wanted
Mr. Cannon to present, he felt it best that he not be identified as
a Church official: "It was the colonel's wish that I should not,
for a time, outwardly assume the presidency of the Eastern mission; he thought that if it were known at first that I occupied
that position, the course he had marked out for me might not be
attended with such good results as it would otherwise be. I therefore requested Bro. Stenhouse [a counselor in the mission presi-
dency] to continue to act as if in charge, and counseled with him
from time to time on the business of the mission."[28]

Public opinion seemed to dictate in large measure what views
editors were willing to express. Therefore, though many agreed
with Elder Cannon concerning the injustice that had frequently
surrounded the reporting on Mormon affairs, they were unwilling to commit themselves to support of the Mormon cause:

There is scarcely one whom I have met who will not coincide with me, after conversing awhile, in regard to the nature of influences, that have been brought to bear against us. They know that most unholy alliances have been formed to accomplish our destruction. Bad as we have been represented, bad as many of them think we are, there is scarcely one who will not avow the opinion that there has been a great amount of falsehood and misrepresentation circulated about us, and that in many instances we have been more sinned against than sinning. But though they express their ideals in private, yet they at present think it would be a costly experiment to give utterance to them in public.[29]

Although they were unwilling to go so far as to support the Mormon cause, they were sometimes willing to speak out for some legislation that would favor the affairs of Utah Territory. President Cannon made visits to editors when any important transactions were being made in Congress for which he hoped to get some public support. He told of his success and failure in getting editors of the *Times* and of the *States* to support a bill concerning territorial rights:

When the time came for the introduction of the bill in Congress, granting to the Territories the right to elect their own officers (afterwards incorporated in the Morris Bill) I had conversations with the leading editors, and sought to enlist their support by setting forth the advantages and good results that would attend the introduction and passage of such a bill; those whose pledges I could not get to support it, I did what I could to induce not to oppose it. . . . Mr. Raymond of the *Times* listened attentively to what I had to say on the subject and agreed that the principle was correct and truly republican and thought it would yet be popular. He afterwards wrote in its favor. . . . Mr. Pryor of the *States*, at first was inclined to be favorable both on this and other points, and made me promises that led me to hope for good results in him; but they were never fulfilled.[30]

In addition to problems with uncooperative editors, Church officials struggled with privacy in their correspondence between Utah and the East. Elder Cannon's suspicions that his mail was being tampered with were apparently confirmed by this vexing experience: "A few weeks ago, I received a letter from one of my relatives, informing me in reply to the surprise I had expressed at not receiving any letters from home, that he himself had written five, besides the other written by my family; the letter which contained this intelligence was the only one of the five I received. Some letters that I have received have borne the marks of having been tampered with. If they would forward them after opening and perusing the contents, it would not be quite so bad as both reading and destroying."[31] The privacy problem became so serious that a code was developed for important communications between the Church leaders in Utah and their representatives in the East, including George Q. Cannon and Thomas L. Kane.[32]

The anti-Mormon element in the East sought vigorously to slant Utah news against the Church and to win editorial support for slander and lies about the Mormons. However, Brother Cannon's efforts seemed to have triumphed at times. In writing to President Young, he observed that there seemed to be a temporary lull in attacks against Utah and the Mormons, and although some attributed this period of quiet to a preoccupation with the war in Europe, he gave this reason: "The fact is, they have been so thoroughly foiled and beaten that they must stop to breathe awhile." As was typical of George Q. Cannon, he recognized the source of this success as being a power beyond his own: "God has held them in derision and all their plans and well-laid schemes have been brought to naught. This is a cause of great encouragement to me, for when I see how little I can accomplish by my puny efforts I am comforted and sustained with the knowledge that our God can by apparently trifling and insignificant means accomplish great results—that He can stay the progress of the wicked and proud, can overrule their measures and cause good results to spring from evil designs and intentions."[33]

Lobbying for Favorable Legislation

Although Elder Cannon's chief political efforts were directed at influencing public opinion through the newspapers, Thomas L. Kane also gave him letters of introduction to congressmen, and he solicited their support for legislation favorable to Utah.[34] His dealings in this regard were of course unofficial, since William H. Hooper was Utah's territorial delegate to Congress.[35] If Elder Cannon entertained any idealism concerning statesmanship in Washington, these illusions were soon dispersed by his firsthand observation of the hard realities of politics: "Party feeling runs high and the interests of the country are completely lost sight of in the desire to benefit the party. The daily scenes in the halls of Congress present a wretched spectacle. No man who loves liberty and free and liberal institutions can witness these things without feeling that the glory of our nation is rapidly fading away—and that should these evils continue the destruction of the government of the United States is inevitable."[36]

Elder Cannon's association with these men of political influence revealed to him that many of them were willing to act against Mormons on the testimonies of people whom they knew to be vile and corrupt: "The part that most of the public men in this nation have taken against us, has been taken with their eyes wide open to the iniquitous character of our accusers, and with the full knowledge of their base and infernal corruptions. There are but few, if indeed any, that can ever plead ignorance on these points; of this I am well satisfied."[37]

Some of the major political concerns Utah faced during Elder Cannon's sojourn in Washington were these: the right of the people in the territory to choose their own officials rather than having federal appointees sent to govern them;[38] the insulting presence of an army in Utah;[39] the proposals to "dismember" the Territory of Utah, i. e., to reduce the size of the territory and exclude some Mormon settlements from it;[40] the proposed measures against freedom of religion, i. e., the practice of plural marriage;[41] and the perennial question of statehood.

Elder Cannon's efforts to turn public opinion in favor of the Mormons on these vital issues would probably not have been nearly so successful without the counsel and influence of Colonel Thomas L. Kane. Not only did he introduce Elder Cannon to editors and congressmen, but also on several occasions he personally visited the president of the United States in behalf of the Mormons. The firsthand information Colonel Kane relayed to Elder Cannon after visiting the chief executive was invaluable to his strategy. President Buchanan's vicarious association with Mormon concerns through Colonel Kane made him feel that he was a friend of the Mormons. Elder Cannon wrote to Brigham Young: "Speaking about President Buchanan reminds me of what Colonel Kane says about him and his feelings towards us; he among all his colleagues thinks he is our best friend and the Col. has thought it best to encourage him in the feeling to some extent, as with his peculiar turn he thinks he would feel a sense of pride in being thought our protector. He says the old man has done well in several instances, better almost than he could have expected, having manifested interest on several occasions in our affairs and in our behalf."[42]

A letter to President Young in the spring of 1860 gives further evidence of President Buchanan's feelings and mentions some specific issues in which he "manifested interest" on behalf of the Mormons:

Our friend [Kane] was here two or three days last week, and had a long, pleasant and satisfactory interview with the President. He thought that he would have to set forth in plainness to His Excellency the danger there would be of another difficulty if certain measures were persisted in: i. e. the dismemberment of the Territory, etc., etc. But he was agreeably disappointed. The old gentleman [Buchanan] launched out immediately and scarcely left him anything to say. The bill against polygamy he was afraid might pass both Houses. He did not want us disturbed, nor any cause of trouble given us, and would use his influence with his friends to have unfriendly and unjust legislation arrested. But every prominent man nearly had his own pet scheme to carry out, and they are not so easily controlled even by him.[43]

President Buchanan evidently respected Kane's opinion a great deal. In July of 1859 some anti-Mormons who felt that Governor Cumming was not hard enough in his treatment of the Mormons got up a lobby to have him removed and replaced by none other than Colonel Albert Sidney Johnston.[44] Thomas Kane heard from a mutual friend that the president seemed willing to yield to the pressures exerted on him by those favoring this shake-up; the president did seem to have some concern, however, about how Colonel Kane would feel about replacing Governor Cumming—whom Colonel Kane liked and who was sympathetic toward the Mormons—with Johnston, whom Kane disliked immensely and had even challenged to a duel at one time.[45]

In order that the president might fully understand Kane's ardent opposition to this proposal, the Colonel accepted an invitation to speak to the Historical Society at New York. He was at that time very ill, and his family and friends implored him not to make the journey; but he was determined in spite of his suffering to let his voice be heard publicly in the interest of maintaining what peace there was in Utah. The Colonel, having made certain that newspaper reporters were present in abundance, delivered a powerful discourse praising Governor Cumming and his administration in Utah and championing the Mormon cause.[46] He achieved his desire: "This colorful, dramatic and sympathetic portrayal of Mormon effort and Mormon suffering had the desired effect to turn the scale in Governor Cumming's favor. President Buchanan had received his answer. . . . Colonel Johnston's budding political career was blighted."[47]

Thus Colonel Kane, "friend of the Mormons," once again intervened and spared the citizens of Utah further governmental abuse. George Q. Cannon was a witness of this noble defense and greatly admired Colonel Kane for delivering it under such physical duress: "I was in the East at the time and familiar with all the circumstances, and I was deeply impressed with the Colonel's conduct on that occasion. I have often thought that probably there was not one Elder in the Church out of a thousand who would have taken such risks or deemed it necessary to have gone to such pains as he did on that occasion to accomplish such an end. I was present at the lecture and saw that he suffered great pain during its delivery. But that was characteristic of the man. When a duty had to be performed he never hesitated about attempting it."[48]

Given such assistance by the Colonel, President Cannon's efforts in the East elicited this recognition from Brigham Young: "Brother George Q. Cannon has been in the States during two years past, and has done all he could to do good to the people of Utah. He has been faithful, has traveled from place to place, and has accomplished all he possibly could."[49]

Elder Cannon's friendship with Colonel Kane continued for many years. In 1883, as Colonel Kane was dying, he instructed his wife to write a letter to the Mormons. In this letter, addressed to George Q. Cannon, who was then in the First Presidency, Mrs. Kane said that her husband's last request was that she "send the sweetest message you can make up to my Mormon friends—to all my dear Mormon friends." She added, "Nothing I could 'make up,' I am persuaded, could be sweeter to you than this evidence that you were in his latest thoughts."[50]

The Colonel's lifelong devotion to the Mormons led to speculation that he was baptized into the Church, but kept his membership a secret in order to maintain his effectiveness as an "objective" defender of the Mormon people. These rumors apparently were unfounded: "The records of the St. George Temple disclose the fact that on the 25th of April, 1884, George Q. Cannon, doubtless the closest friend of Colonel Kane after Brigham Young, was baptized for him and also received the endowments for him on the same occasion; so that it seems clear that Colonel Kane was never a member of the Church during his lifetime."[51]

Gathering to Zion

Because all the Utah elders had been called home in consequence of the "invasion" of Johnston's army, missionary work in
the Eastern States was nearly at a standstill at the time Elder
Cannon was called to preside. In fact, says the mission history,
"in 1858, there was no general organization of the Church in
the Eastern States. All of the Zion Elders having been called
home, local brethren were called to take charge."[52] During Elder
Cannon's presidency, little change was made in this direction.
His efforts were expended more toward gathering the Saints to
Zion than toward establishing a "general organization" in the
East. The doctrine of gathering had been an integral part of the
Restoration since the time the Church was organized. In Octo-
ber of 1830, the Lord revealed his will to the Prophet Joseph
Smith concerning those who would accept the restored gospel:

> And even so will I gather mine elect from the four quarters of the
> earth, even as many as will believe in me, and hearken unto my
> voice.[53]

And a few months later,

> And it shall come to pass that the righteous shall be gathered out
> from among all nations, and shall come to Zion, singing with
> songs of everlasting joy.[54]

Commenting upon these prophecies, President Cannon observed: "A remarkable feature, something unheard of, that the
principles of this religion when preached should have the effect
to gather out from every nation, kindred, tongue and people

those who espoused them. Yet every word has been fulfilled. Wherever the Elders of this Church have gone they have gone accompanied by that wonderful power, the power of gathering the people together; not of one race, not of one language, but people of every race and of every language, showing the adaptability of its principles to the people of the frozen north as well as to those of the torrid south."[55] He further pointed out that gathering to Zion was not a result of pressure from the missionaries: "It has not been the inducement of the Elder; . . . it has not been any influence of this character that they have sought to wield over the people that has gathered them together. They have come of their own accord. They have forsaken home, friends, old associations, ancestral tombs, and everything of this character that is calculated to bind men to their native land; they have severed all these and have gathered out and cast their lots with the people of their faith in these mountains."[56]

To those who did not understand the power of the Holy Ghost, the inexplicable desire to gather to Zion that welled up in the hearts of nearly all converts immediately after their baptism must have seemed mystical indeed: "After baptism by immersion . . . came the baptism of desire, a strange and irresistible longing which ravished them and filled them with a nostalgia for Zion, their common home. . . . 'Gathering' came to be regarded as the sign of one's faithfulness, and the convert who did not feel the pull was considered a queer fish in the gospel net."[57]

One British missionary described the "pull" in these words:

Verily there is power in Mormonism. People who once felt they would rather die than leave "happy England," who used to sing "Happy Land" and "Britons Never Shall Be Slaves," who looked upon other countries with supreme contempt . . . now perceive that they have been in bondage, in darkness, and in Babylon, and sing with joyful hearts—

> There is a land beyond the sea
> Where I should like to be;
> And dearer far than all the rest,
> Is that bright land to be . . . [58]

Besides the spiritual rewards of gathering to Zion, President Cannon also promised the Saints that they would be better off in other ways, including even their physical appearance: "Transplanting the Saints to Zion will benefit in every way if they will do right. With all the rest, their physical beauty will be increased. They are already strong and robust, but handsome forms and faces will . . . become common. The heavenly influence of the Spirit of the Lord, with more favorable circumstances and a more generous diet, will effect this."[59]

When the Saints finally found a more isolated home of their own, relatively free from persecutions, the Church increased efforts to gather the honest in heart from all nations to Zion. President Brigham Young wrote in a general epistle to the Saints, "We will soon send Elders abroad by hundreds and thousands to harvest souls among the nations, and the inhabitants of the earth shall speedily hear of the salvation prepared by Israel's God for his people."[60] The scope of this gathering is evident in the far-flung missionary calls given at the general conferences of the Church during this period in Utah: "A special two day conference was commenced in G. S. L. C.: 106 Elders were called to go on missions, namely 6 to the United States, 4 to Nova Scotia and the British N. A. provinces, 2 to British Guiana (So. America), 4 to the West Indies, 39 to Great Britain, 1 to France, 4 to

Germany, 3 to Prussia, 2 to Gibraltar, 1 to Denmark, 2 to Nor-
way, 9 to Calcutta and Hindostan, 4 to China, 3 to Siam, 3 to
Cape of Good Hope, Africa, 10 to Australia, and 9 to the
Hawaiian Islands."[61]

As thousands of converts were baptized into the Church, the
missionaries and Church leaders emphasized the need to gather
to Zion. President Young described the condition of the Church
and his hopes for the kingdom they were establishing in the
mountains:

> We have been kicked out of the frying-pan into the fire, out
> of the fire into the middle of the floor, and here we are and here
> we will stay. God has shown me that this is the spot to locate his
> people, and here is where they will prosper. . . .
>
> As the Saints gather here and get strong enough to posses the
> land, God will temper the climate and we shall build a city and a
> temple to the Most High God in this place. We will extend our
> settlements to the east and west, to the north and to the south,
> and we will build towns and cities by the hundreds, and thousands
> of Saints will gather in from the nations of the earth. This will
> become the great highway of nations.[62]

And so the call was made: "The voice of the 'Good Shepherd' is
to all Saints, even to the ends of the earth; gather yourselves together, come home . . . will you listen to the voice of the 'Good
Shepherd'? . . . Will you be obedient to the heavenly commandments?"[63] The doctrine of gathering was taught as a "heavenly
commandment," not just as a suggestion. Writing on the subject
in the *Western Standard,* Elder Cannon had declared: "The Lord
has commanded his people to gather themselves together—
to come out of Babylon, that they might not be partakers of
her sins, and that they might receive not of her plagues. This

commandment is as binding in its time and season, and as necessary to be obeyed to insure the favor and approbation of our Father in heaven, as the commandment to believe in the Lord Jesus,
to repent, and be baptized."[64]

Because the great majority of the conversions took place in
the British Isles and Western Europe, most of those who gathered were from these countries. For many years the emigration
route from Europe to Nauvoo, and later to the Great Salt Lake
Valley, was the same route George Cannon and his family had
taken—to New Orleans and up the Mississippi or Missouri
Rivers. In 1854, President Brigham Young announced that the
port of disembarkation would be changed from New Orleans to
Philadelphia, Boston, or New York. The reason for this change
was that the Saints traveling inland on the rivers were almost uni-
versally plagued with various diseases. Another reason for this
change was that railroads had been built from these eastern cities
toward the West, and the Saints could now take passage on these
trains to the frontier.[65] In writing to the Saints in England, President Young counseled them to "pursue the Northern route
from Boston, New York or Philadelphia, and land at Iowa City
or the then terminus of the railroad."[66] In this same letter, he
said, "We propose sending men of faith and experience to some
proper outfitting point" to assist the Saints in reaching the valley. President Cannon's calling as mission president included the
position of chief emigration officer for the Church. His duties
included "outfitting" the Saints for the trek to Zion as mentioned by Brigham Young.

Most of the Saints arrived at the eastern seaports in vessels
chartered by Church emigration officials in England. President
Cannon arranged to have these Saints met and boarded onto
trains bound for the frontier. The unpredictable nature of sea

travel sometimes caused inconvenient delays for those meeting the emigrants. Writing about five hundred Saints whom Elder Cannon had shepherded to St. Joseph, Missouri, he reported to President Young "They are late, having been detained three weeks in Liverpool, waiting for the 'William Tapscott,' and when about three weeks out they had the small pox break out which caused their detention in quarantine in New York for several days. Twelve of the Saints had to be left there."[67]

The Mormon emigrants had a reputation among English seamen for being exceptionally well disciplined and clean. The Saints made a similar impression on railroad officials while traveling to the frontier: "The credit that is usually given to our people crossing the sea was not withheld on the car; they were called a superior class of emigrants, and many of the Railway Agents told me they had never seen so large a body of emigrants come right from shipboard so cleanly."[68]

At the railroad terminus, the Church emigration agents met the Saints and outfitted them for the thousand-mile journey to Zion. President Cannon was involved in the business of purchasing oxen, wagons, provisions, and even handcarts for the travelers. In 1860, President Cannon was responsible for sending two handcart companies numbering 349 souls to Utah. They were the last of more than 3,000 Saints who reached Zion in this manner.[69] The Journal History recorded his efforts to procure supplies as cheaply as possible for the emigrants: "Brother Cannon stated that he had been to the frontier to make arrangements for the emigration this spring. He thinks that the emigrants can be furnished with handcarts, wagons, teams, etc., a little cheaper than last year."[70]

President Cannon's business connections were so extensive that Brigham Young said, "George Q. is known from St. Joseph to St. Louis and in the East in connection with our business and trading."[71] However, his concern was not alone for the physical arrangements of their journey, but also for spiritual guidance and instruction. President Brigham Young made it clear that gathering to the valley would necessitate much sacrifice on the part of the Saints:

> We have been willing to live on bread and water, and many times very little bread too, for years, that we might search out and plant the Saints in a goodly land. This we have accomplished. . . . Therefore, let all who can procure a bit of bread, and one garment on their back, be assured there is water plenty and pure by the way, and doubt no longer, but come next year to the place of gathering, even in flocks, as doves fly to their windows before a storm.[72]

At times the spirit of prophecy even allowed President Cannon to make comforting promises to his westbound brothers and sisters. Oscar O. Stoddard, the captain of one of the two last handcart companies, recorded such an occasion in his journal: "I cannot remember the number of souls who were in the company at the start, but Brother Cannon told them if they would be humble and faithful, not one of them should die on the road to the Valley; which was literally fulfilled as everyone who started from Florence with us came into Salt Lake City."[73]

Many of the emigrants were assisted by the Perpetual Emigration Fund (PEF) which President Young had established in 1849. Voluntary donations provided the means whereby the PEF could loan poor Saints enough capital to come to Zion. The beneficiaries of this aid (over fifty thousand people in its nearly forty years of operation) agreed to pay back the borrowed funds so that others could receive the same blessing.[74] Because repayment often took years, there was always a greater demand on the fund than it could supply, and consequently many Saints who longed to come to Zion had to wait for years. Elder Cannon wrote to President Young concerning some members in the East who suffered these circumstances: "There are poor persons in the various branches who have no earthly prospect of getting away if left to fit themselves out whom I am trying to arrange plans to assist out. Many of them have been for many years members of the Church, and they express themselves willing to do anything or put up with any inconvenience if they can only have their heart's desire—reach Zion."[75]

Elder Cannon's desire to help the poor reach the valley spawned an idea that revolutionized the process of getting the Saints from the frontier to Utah. He presented this idea to Brigham Young: "I have thought that a good many of the poor Saints might be taken through who would otherwise have to remain, if they (the emigrants) could go through with part rations and be met with teams with provisions from the Valley . . . instead of hauling flour such a distance, as they would have to do did they take a full supply from the Missouri River."[76]

Acting upon this suggestion, in April of 1860 President Young sent his nephew, Joseph W. Young, to the railroad terminus with thirty-six wagons loaded with flour and supplies. Not only were the supplies given out, but the poorer emigrants were transported back to Utah in the wagons. They arrived on October 3, 1860, completing the first one-season round trip made by a wagon train from the Valley.[77] A few weeks later, Joseph Young preached a sermon in the Tabernacle on "oxteamology," the art of keeping oxen in good enough condition to complete a two-thousand mile journey in one season.[78] This method of transporting Saints proved so successful that these Church trains almost entirely eliminated the expensive operation of outfitting each Saint with his own team and wagon. During the next nine years, until the coming of the railway, nearly 2,000 wagons went East with 2,389 "wagon missionaries," and conveyed back to Utah more than 20,000 emigrants.[79] During President Cannon's nearly two years as emigration agent, he was responsible for assisting thousands of faithful Saints in their gathering to Zion.

The Call to Apostleship

The most significant event that transpired during President Cannon's Eastern States mission was the fulfillment of the prophecy Parley P. Pratt had spoken four years earlier, declaring that George Q. Cannon would become a member of the Quorum of the Twelve and fill the vacancy left by Apostle Pratt's passing.[80] In May 1857, while Elder Pratt was on a mission to the Southern States and in the prime of his service to the Lord's kingdom, an assassin's bullet cut him down. During a meeting of the First Presidency and the Twelve held in the Historian's Office on October 23, 1859, President Brigham Young said, "I nominate George Q. Cannon to be a member of the Twelve."[81] The others present at the meeting accepted this proposal, and Elder Cannon was notified by letter of this high calling. On the 13th of December, he wrote to President Brigham Young his acceptance of this responsibility and expressed the feelings of his heart on the subject:

> I know that I scarcely need say to you how peculiar my feelings were on reading in your letter of my appointment to fill the vacancy in the quorum of the Twelve, occasioned by the death of Bro. Parley. You know, I am sure, much better what they were and are than I can write them. I had to steal aside to give vent to my

feelings and hide the tremor that shook my frame. I trembled with fear and dread, and yet I was filled with joy—fear and dread when I reflected on my weakness and unworthiness and the great responsibility that rested upon one holding the apostleship, and joy to think of the goodness and favor of the Lord and the love and confidence of my brethren. May the Lord give me grace and strength to magnify this Holy Priesthood and calling to the glory of His name and the salvation of His Israel, is my earnest prayer.[82]

Elder Cannon's feelings of inadequacy apparently led him to reflect on the passage of scripture that had sustained him as a young missionary in the Sandwich Islands and as a struggling editor in San Francisco. He trusted that the Lord would prepare a way for him to accomplish the thing which he had been commanded (see 1 Nephi 3:7). In writing to his Uncle John Taylor, now his colleague in the Quorum of the Twelve, Elder Cannon expressed his faith:

The assurance that I have the confidence and good feelings of my brethren, has sustained me very much since hearing of the appointment to which you allude. My own weakness, and inability to discharge the duties of such an important office and calling, were so apparent to me that I trembled at the thought of it. I know, however, that our Heavenly Father never calls one of His children to perform any duty or to occupy any station, without endowing him with every qualification, if he will but seek after them in the right spirit.[83]

Although George was a young man with many talents and abilities and a great desire to succeed in all that he did, he apparently did not aspire to a high position, either in the world or in the Church. Referring to his childhood desire to be "a standard bearer of the gospel," an elder in the Church, he said: "I have never had a desire in my heart for any other office in the world, civil, political, or ecclesiastical. I would have been content to be an Elder, and to have remained in that capacity and to have held the privilege of preaching the gospel. Yet the Lord saw fit to choose me to be an Apostle."[84]

Brother Pratt's prophecy, now fulfilled, of George Q. Cannon's call to this high position in the Church must not have been the first indication Elder Cannon had concerning his future apostleship, for he indicated that he had this premonition in his youth and had often prayed that he might be freed from this awesome calling:

> The Lord revealed to me when I was quite young that I at some time would be an Apostle. I never told it to any human being; but on more than one occasion I have gone out and besought the Lord to choose some one else and relieve me of that responsibility. I have besought Him earnestly, time and again, that if I could only get my salvation and exaltation without being called to that high and holy responsibility, I would much rather He would choose some other person.[85]

In the April general conference of 1860, Brigham Young presented George Q. Cannon's name to the general assembly of the Church for their sustaining vote:

> The First Presidency and the Quorum of the Twelve have made choice of George Q. Cannon to fill the vacancy in the Quorum of the Twelve. He is pretty generally known by the people. He has been raised in the Church, and was one of our promising Elders in the Sandwich Islands. He went upon that mission when he was

quite young. He is also known by many as the editor of a paper which he published in California, called *The Western Standard*. He is now East, assisting in the transaction of business and taking charge of this year's emigration. I will present his name to the congregation to become a member of the Quorum of the Twelve, to fill the vacancy occasioned by the death of Parley Parker Pratt. If this is pleasing to you, you will be so kind as to vote accordingly. (The vote was unanimous).[86]

Of course, Elizabeth and Sarah Jane Cannon were among the congregation and raised their hands to sustain their husband in his new calling as an Apostle of the Lord.

In early June, two fellow members of the Quorum of the Twelve, Amasa M. Lyman and Charles C. Rich, visited with Elder Cannon in Florence, Nebraska, on their way to preside over the European Mission. Already impressed with Elder Cannon in their former associations, they sent this evaluation of his labors back to the Valley: "Brother Cannon was very busy in preparing the emigrants for the plains, in which he has thus far been eminently successful."[87] A few weeks later, Elder Cannon was instructed to return to the Valley after an absence of nearly two years. His family had nearly doubled in size while he was gone, with the births of Frank Jenne Cannon, born to Sarah Jane, January 25, 1859, and of Abraham Hoagland Cannon, born to Elizabeth, March 12, 1859. In future years, Frank became the first senator from the State of Utah, and Abraham a member of the Quorum of the Twelve Apostles.[88]

A few days after his reunion with his family, Brother Cannon was ordained to the Council of the Twelve. On August 26, 1860, at 5:00 p.m., in the Church Historian's Office, President Young bestowed the keys and powers of the apostolic calling on Elder Cannon:

Brother George Quayle Cannon, in the name of Jesus Christ, and
in the virtue of the Holy Priesthood, we the servants of the Lord
Jesus Christ, lay our hands upon your head to ordain you and set
you apart to be an apostle of the Lord Jesus Christ in this last dispensation, an apostle and witness that Joseph Smith, Jun., was
called of God and sent forth to the children of men to establish
the kingdom of God on the earth for the last time, that kingdom
which should grow and multiply and increase until it should fill
the whole earth and overpower every other kingdom upon the
earth and bring in subjection to the will of Christ the nations of
the earth.[89]

CHAPTER 7

The European Mission

The Mission in Great Britain

ON SEPTEMBER 27, 1860, only a month after his return
to his mountain home, George Q. Cannon demonstrated once
again his unswerving dedication to the cause of preaching the
gospel of Jesus Christ and building the latter-day kingdom of
God. On this date, newly ordained as an Apostle, Elder Cannon departed for the fifth time in ten years for a mission of un-
determined duration—this time to Great Britain. Although
this young wife, Sarah Jane, had only enjoyed the blessing of his
association for a little more than a total of six months since
their marriage two and a half years before, it was decided that

The dock at
Plymouth, England,
ca. 1863

Elizabeth should accompany their husband on this mission. Sarah Jane was an excellent spinner, capable of supporting herself and little Frank by her own labors. George and Elizabeth planned to take three-year-old John Q. and eighteen-month-old Abraham to England with them, but during a visit to the Cannons' temporary home President Brigham Young gave them some inspired counsel. He advised them to leave Elizabeth's two sons home with Sarah Jane and promised them that if they did the boys would be safe and well upon their return. Of course they heeded this counsel.[1]

The specific assignment of this mission was for President Cannon to join the two Apostles Amasa M. Lyman and Charles C. Rich in presiding over the European Mission, with headquarters in Liverpool, England. These two Apostles had preceded President Cannon to the mission field, arriving in England on July 27, 1860.[2] Their assignment was detailed in this short letter of instruction from the Presidency of the Church:

> We authorize and wish you, upon your arrival in Liverpool, England, to take the Presidency of the Mission in the British Isles and counsel, control, and regulate all persons, business, and affairs pertaining to that mission and all the missions connected therewith, whether in Europe, Asia, Africa, or the islands of the sea, according to the dictates of the holy Spirit to you, and such counsel as you may from time to time receive from the first Presidency of the Church.[3]

Calling three Apostles to preside over the mission indicated the importance the leaders of the Church placed on the work in Europe. These three men brought with them a wealth of talent: "Elder Lyman was doubtless the most persuasive and forceful speaker in the Church at that time; Elder Rich, one of the wisest counselors and most faithful and earnest teachers of the plain truths of the gospel, and the practical duties of the saints; while Elder Cannon was the clearest and most forceful writer in the Church."[4]

President Cannon's specific assignments in this triumvirate were to take charge of the mission's printing business, to publish the *Millennial Star,* and to oversee emigration. When President Brigham Young ordained George Q. Cannon an Apostle, he also set him apart for this mission to England:

> And inasmuch as you are called to go forth to England to take charge of the Church business there and of the printing there and of the emigration from there we pray our Father in Heaven to give you wisdom, strength and power to magnify your calling and walk in all prudence and faith before your brethren, and to be equal with your brethren of the Twelve in all things in holding the keys of this ministry and power to all nations, first to the gentiles and then to the Jews as they shall be grafted in again, and to all Israel to the uttermost points of the earth.[5]

President and Sister Cannon left Great Salt Lake City in the early fall in charge of a company of thirty-five other missionaries bound for the British Isles.[6] Two weeks later, writing ahead to Presidents Lyman and Rich from Florence, Nebraska, President Cannon described the good conditions in the beautiful mountain home that he was called to leave again: "Everything in the Valley . . . was in a prosperous condition; crops good and bountiful, peace abounding, and the spirit enjoyed copiously by the faithful."[7] President and Sister Cannon arrived in New York City in early December and there visited with two other members of the Twelve, Erastus Snow and Orson Pratt. The Cannons sailed for Southampton, England, on the steamship *Arago,* on

December 8, 1860; and after a safe voyage of thirteen days they set foot on George's native English soil.[8]

The European Mission over which President Cannon presided with Presidents Rich and Lyman consisted of six missions: the Scandinavian Mission, comprising Denmark, Norway, and Sweden; the Swiss Mission, including Switzerland, Italy, and Germany; the French Mission, including France and Belgium; the Netherlands Mission; the British Mission, including England, Ireland, Scotland, and Wales; and the faraway South African Mission.[9] Of these missions, England was by far the most fruitful. Since the commencement of missionary work there in 1837, over 80,000 souls had been baptized into the Church, nearly 20,000 of whom had emigrated to Zion. Some had died and many others had apostatized, leaving about 50,000 members at the time of President Cannon's arrival.[10] He found most of these members extremely poor: "There are very few of the Saints that have any means more than a bare living. Those who have had means have either emigrated or apostatized, leaving the poorest of the Church behind."[11]

The desire of the members to go to Zion in spite of their poverty touched President Cannon's heart. He wrote to President Young, "The Saints are very anxious to emigrate, and cry earnestly to the Lord for deliverance. Since I have been here, I have almost wished that I had means of my own to assist the poor creatures that are destitute and yet so anxious to gather."[12] But President Cannon realized that helping these poor people to reach Zion would not bring worthy results in all cases: "Many of them, I presume if they were picked up and gathered would repay in ingratitude and, in some instances, curses; but there would be some probably who would do right and whose salvation would remunerate for all expended on themselves and the worthless ones."[13] Over the next four years, President Cannon was able to fulfill his desire to help these impoverished English Saints reach Zion in the discharge of his duties as emigration agent.

Because of the conflict between the Northern and Southern States, political relations between the United States and Great Britain were at a low ebb throughout President Cannon's mission. He sometimes wrote home about the poverty in England resulting from the difficulties they had trading with the States: "There is a great amount of distress among the poor in this country at the present time. Thousands upon thousands are out of employ, and strong appeals are being made to the charity of the wealthy to extend relief to them. The stoppage of orders from the States has aggravated the evils already in existence."[14]

In correspondence with President Young, President Cannon noted the materialistic concerns of many Englishmen in regard to the conflict: "The condition of affairs in America is the topic of conversation in these countries. Men already begin to surmise and indulge in fits of wonder as to the probable consequences of the outbreak. Their principal cause for fear is the disastrous effect it will no doubt have upon the trade and commerce of the country; no thought of the probability of a higher being than man having any purpose in view with regard to it, is entertained."[15] In the same letter, President Cannon referred to the notoriety of Joseph Smith's prediction of the war between the states:[16] "The prophecy of Joseph has gained access to some of the journals of this country and those works of the Church containing it are making a pretty rapid sale."[17] Brigham Young's letters to President Cannon contained gloomy indications that this prophecy would be fulfilled: "By last night's pony, we learn that the excitement in the States is constantly waxing fiercer, all

parties merging under the geographical distinction of North and
South, and with increasing bitterness taking sides in accordance
with said geographical party line, with every prospect of their
speedily precipitating themselves into civil war."[18]

During the remainder of President Cannon's mission, while
the Civil War raged, many feared for America's survival, but
George Q. Cannon's faith in his nation's destiny was unshaken.
He prophesied: "America, will yet emerge from the dreadful difficulties in which she is now involved and will yet obtain that position which has been designed by God for her to hold. She will
yet occupy the chief place among the nations and enjoy a form
of government that will be copied, as a model, by surrounding
peoples."[19]

George Q. Cannon's call to the mission presidency de-
manded a full measure of the tact and diplomacy for which he
was becoming well known. At age thirty-three and newly ordained to the Quorum of the Twelve, he was assigned to work
with Elder Lyman, who was fourteen years his senior and who
had eighteen years more experience as an Apostle. Elder Rich
was eighteen years older than President Cannon and had served
in the Quorum of the Twelve for eleven years. In spite of these
differences in age and experience, President Young had assigned
to President Cannon tasks that gave him the most executive responsibility:

> My position was a delicate one, and with some men might have
> been very embarrassing. The duties laid upon me were those usually
> assigned to the senior Apostle, where there was more than one in
> the same field. Those who have any acquaintance with that mission
> can easily understand how easy it would be for men to get up feel-
> ings under such circumstances as we were in, especially when it is
> borne in mind that I was applied to by them, and by all the Elders

in the mission, for information concerning emigration, the management of funds and everything which belonged to the general affairs of the mission. I was by many years the junior, and had only recently been ordained an Apostle, but during the time we labored together in this relationship, neither from Brother Charles C. Rich, nor from Amasa M. Lyman, was there a word or look that could be construed into dissatisfaction with the arrangement.[20]

During the year and a half in which these two apostles were in the mission presidency with him, President Cannon developed an even greater love and respect for them. Of President Lyman he said, "Amasa M. Lyman displayed a magnanimity and freedom from jealousy that I shall never forget." And in speaking of Apostle Rich he wrote: "Charles C. Rich was a man that would do his best in any position that might be assigned him. Other men might have had more intellectual ability than he; but he possessed in all relations of life that goodness of character which is the chief element of greatness and made him the useful and prominent man that he was. His life is one that furnishes an excellent example to the rising generation in Zion."[21]

Not only was President Cannon the junior of the other mission presidents, but he was also younger than many of the missionaries who were called to labor under his direction. Because of the respect that his leadership ability commanded, he had few, if any, problems relating to his youth.

Publishing the *Millennial Star*

President Cannon's time and efforts were divided into three areas of concentration: publishing work, missionary labors, and emigration affairs. This first portion of his labor involved issuing the *Millennial Star,* one of the most powerful missionary tools and aids to the British Saints. This paper had been published monthly, semimonthly, and finally weekly since 1840. George Q. Cannon doubtless enjoyed reading many of its first issues as a boy in England. Its title implies its lofty mission:

> The *Millennial Star* will stand aloof from the common political and commercial news of the day. Its columns will be devoted to the spread of the fulness of the gospel—the restoration of the ancient principles of Christianity—the gathering of Israel—the rolling forth of the kingdom of God among the nations—the signs of the times—the fulfillment of prophecy—recording the judgments of God as they befall the nations, whether signs in the heavens or in the earth, "blood, fire, or vapor of smoke"—in short, whatever is shown forth indicative of the coming of the "Son of Man" and ushering in of his universal reign upon the earth.[22]

In assuming the editorship of the *Star*, President Cannon maintained the paper's noble ideals. The *Deseret News* reported: "Elder Cannon entered upon his duties, as Editor of the *Star*, with the commencement of the current volume. His introductory address breathes the spirit that he had possessed, that of devotedness to the cause of truth, in the dissemination of the principles of which he has constantly been engaged."[23]

During the previous two decades various English firms had done the printing of the *Star* and other Church publications in England, but because of President Cannon's printing experience in Nauvoo, San Francisco, and Fillmore, and because President Young so instructed, Brother Cannon purchased a press, type, and necessary machinery and materials to establish a printing office for the Church in England.[24] This was a bold undertaking, considering that for the last five years the mission had been struggling to pay off a debt of nearly $34,000 to the various printers of the *Millennial Star*.[25] Reporting to President Brigham Young in May of 1861, President Cannon wrote, "The printing office is now under full headway. Upon taking everything into consideration I concluded it would be better to drive our printing machine by steam, and so bought and put up a small engine and boiler."[26] He then detailed some of the problems involved in getting employees for the print shop: "I have been compelled to employ mostly gentile printers, which I do not like; we have a few in the Church; but they are in the ministry, and can ill be spared." He also had trouble getting the ones he did hire to earn their pay: "My patience has been much tried with the old-fogy, time-killing mode of working they have in this country. The usual way of hiring men is by the day. I have tried to have them work by the piece, as under the day system, they require so much watching; they will 'sojer.'"[27]

In spite of these and other difficulties, editor Cannon reported: "We have now issued from this Office seven nos. of the 'Star': three nos. of the 'Journal' [*Journal of Discourses*] and eight nos. of the 'Udgorn Seion' [*Zion's Trumpet*, published in the Welsh language]."[28]

Another problem relating to President Cannon's publishing work involved an enormous excess of books and pamphlets that had accumulated over the years. These works had been printed in huge quantities in order to obtain cheaper rates. Writing to President Young, he lamented "having 2,590 volumes of Sister E. R. Snow's poems, 19 having been sold in three years" and 3,464 copies of "The Harp of Zion," 21 having been sold in the same period of time. "There are editions of some works, which at the ration they have been sold during the past three years will take half the millennium to sell."

President Cannon then suggested a plan for their disposal: "Were they mine, I would think it better to sell them to the Saints and those disposed to buy our works at the price of waste paper or even give them away than to have them lie year after year rotting on the shelves or in boxes doing no good to anybody."[29] Apparently this program was adopted. A letter to President Young six months later contained this report: "The large stock of pamphlets that we were burdened with I am glad to say is decreasing very rapidly. They are, from what I can learn, being liberally circulated among the people of the Church."[30]

In addition to the books, pamphlets, and periodicals published under President Cannon's supervision, he secured President Young's permission to publish a volume of editorials from the *Western Standard.* This work was accomplished "without using any Church funds, or without calling upon the Saints for any, or in any manner interfering with the work of the ministry."[31] This volume, *Writings from the "Western Standard,"* was not published with the aim to make money, but because he felt these editorials might have "value in my children's eyes in the years to come" and be instrumental in showing them the "senseless opposition which had to be met, in the preaching of the Gospel of Jesus in its fulness and the building up of Zion according to the revelations of the Almighty."[32]

Another printing project President Cannon undertook was to edit and republish the hymnal used at that time. Typical of his diplomacy, President Cannon asked President Young to criticize and correct the old hymn book, thinking it better not to change it himself for fear he would insult the Saints who had compiled the original edition. He did, however, send along a couple of his own recommendations for change: "There is one hymn (35th, p. 46) which was written by an Elder who is now an apostate, and a very bitter and deadly enemy of the Church. Shall his prayer be preserved in our book?"[33] President Cannon also took the liberty to make alterations in a hymn that contained the words "The mountains, the mountains, the mountains sublime, / Covered over with Saints, milk, honey and wine." While some members may have objected to the wine, his only justification for changing this hymn was that it "always makes me think of buckwheat cakes."[34]

Although the printing office was involved with many other projects, the weekly publication of the *Millennial Star* was still the most important and demanding of President Cannon's duties. Besides conducting a great deal of mission business through its pages, he used the *Star* to instruct, preach, and prophesy. An example of his instructions to the elders appeared in print February 15, 1862:

> Every Elder who lays his hands upon a child to bless it should be careful that he is not led by fancy, or by a desire to say some wonderful things, instead of being prompted by the Spirit of the Lord. For when the Spirit of the Lord does not dictate, however many blessings an Elder may promise and fine things he may say, disappointment is sure to follow. The parents of the child have their expectations raised only to be dashed again to the earth. It is too often the case that in blessing children the Elders entertain the idea that they ought to pronounce upon its head every good thing they can think of.[35]

President Cannon capitalized on the terror of the Civil War and England's concern in the matter by writing many editorials about the judgments of God predicted for nations that reject His messengers of truth. He taught that the Lord was avenging the deaths of Joseph and Hyrum by allowing the Civil War to scourge the United States: "There is no sin that a nation can commit, which the Lord avenges so speedily and fearfully as he does the shedding of innocent blood, or, in other words, the killing of his anointed and authorized servants."[36]

Of course, President Cannon did not speak of wars and judgments without proclaiming the road to peace:

> War is one of the scourges which man, by his sinfulness, has brought upon himself. There is one way—and but one way—to avert it and that is for the people to obey God's commands, through whose power alone can this and other threatened evils be stayed. This is too simple for the great men of the earth to believe. Like their class in every preceding generation, they view such a proposition as ridiculous and treat it with contempt, practically asserting, by their actions, that they consider their wisdom and plans as being infinitely superior to the Lord's.[37]

Besides instruction and prophecy, President Cannon waxed eloquent in declaring some of the sublime concepts of Mormonism, such as man's divine origin and potential destiny:

> There was a period when we, with Jesus and others, basked in the light of the presence of God and enjoyed His smiles. We are the children of God, and as His children, there is no attribute we ascribe to Him that we do not possess, though they may be dormant or in embryo. The mission of the Gospel is to develop these powers and make us like our Heavenly Parent. I know this is true, and such knowledge makes me feel happy.[38]

Overseeing the Missionary Work

Besides his printing duties, President Cannon spent a great

deal of time working with the Saints and missionaries in the preaching of the gospel. One of his first proselytizing efforts was to visit his own relatives on the Isle of Man and in Liverpool. Although he found them full of prejudice against his message, he was able to make their acquaintance and gather information that could later be used for genealogical purposes.

President Cannon had a deep conviction of the value of missionary work, not only for those who received the gospel through it but also for those who served as missionaries. He considered traveling without purse or scrip, as the missionaries did in those days, a marvelous blessing to them:

> Elders of this Church differ from all others. They go out without purse and scrip, relying upon the Lord, putting their trust in him, devoting their time, their energies, and the ability that God has given unto them for the purpose of enlightening their fellow-men concerning that which they know to be the truth. I do not know any greater evidence than this that men could give to their fellow-men of their sincerity. And when men go forth in this way they are very likely to live so that the spirit of the mighty God of Jacob will be with them. . . . When a man is hungry, when he is without money, when he has no friends, he is very apt to feel after some Being that has power; if he has any faith in God he is very apt to exercise it, and by the constant exercise of that faith, if he did not know before he went upon his mission that God lives, that God is near, that he hears and answers prayers, he would be very likely to learn these things.[39]

His strong feelings on the value of serving a mission were based on his own experiences as a young missionary in Hawaii: "It was in this manner that I learned most convincingly in my youth that this was the work of God. I believed it, yes, I may say

I knew it to be true, but when I was sent out as a missionary without purse and scrip and compelled to feel after God and ask Him for those things that I wanted, I learned to my entire satisfaction that when I did need God's blessings He was at hand to confer them upon me."[40]

President Cannon expected from the missionaries under his care the same standards of self-discipline, exactness, and excellence that he had maintained during his service to the Lord. He saw to it that all his clerks became "excellent penmen" and that all his missionaries were dressed in a manner befitting their noble calling. "Each Elder should be clad in a full suit of black, of clerical cut, and surmounted by a tall silk hat."[41]

His vast experience in being guided by the Spirit of the Lord in his preaching, coupled with the fact that he had once been afraid to face an audience, enabled him to speak with authority to the elders about preaching by the Spirit. He knew how readily fear could thwart the flow of the Spirit, and he explained this danger: "If the spirit of fear has the mastery, the Spirit of God is checked, and the man is not able to tell the people the will and counsel of the Lord."[42] He told his missionaries how they could obtain the Spirit of the Lord in their preaching and promised them all that they could become powerful under its influence: "When the Spirit of God takes possession of a man, and he will yield to its influence, it will take away all fear and enable him to tell the truth in great plainness; and if he will persevere, nothing doubting, we dare promise every Elder that he will be able to overcome his feelings of fear and embarrassment, and be filled with holy boldness to declare the gospel unto the people in whose midst he is appointed to labor."[43]

President Cannon constantly warned the elders against evils that would prevent the operation of the Spirit in their work.

Chief among these sins, he felt, was unchastity: "I am convinced that the lust after women is a sin that has been very common, and has, like the commission of adultery, resulted in every instance in the loss of the Spirit and there is great necessity to warn the Elders against it."[44] President Cannon was very specific in declaring the consequences that would eventually come to the elders as a result of unchaste thoughts and the loss of the Spirit: "If Elders allow their thoughts to wander after women, they will sooner or later, unless they speedily repent, find themselves covered with shame and condemnation, and the result will be that through their lusts they will be led to the terrible condition of apostasy. . . . I can prophesy that the Elder who indulges in this sin will be led to destruction."[45]

Widespread sexual immorality was a serious problem among some missionaries from Zion and among many local elders and Saints. Only a few weeks after his arrival, George Q. Cannon wrote to President Young: "There has been a fearful amount of sin indulged in by Elders here which is now coming to light. The spirit of whoredom has been rife."[46] Through personal interviews with local elders, President Cannon discovered that serious transgressions had been committed by "no less than seventeen, some of them presidents of conferences and all of them engaged in the ministry." All of these, he assured President Young, had been "dealt with" for their sin. President Cannon expressed his dedication to discharging his duty as mission president and as an Apostle of the Lord in warning the people: "I feel determined by the help of the Lord to do all in my power to solemnly warn my brethren of the Priesthood and the Saints of the consequence that will attend the commission of sin . . . that I may be able in the day of the Lord Jesus Christ to stand before Him with my garments unspotted with the blood of men."[47] He realized that the success of the mission depended on curbing evil: "We feel that as iniquity is exposed and uprooted the power of God will be experienced to an extent not known at present."[48]

Another disappointing situation President Cannon faced on a few occasions on his mission was missionary misuse of Church-collected funds. He apologized for having to report this to President Young: "I find that many Elders have been very careless, to call it by no worse name, respecting finances. I do not like to say anything to you about the evil actions of the brethren; but it is necessary sometimes that you should be informed."[49] He bemoaned the fact that some of the elders simply could not be trusted to live the commandments on their own: "Many of the Elders who ought to be men capable of leading the people in the paths of salvation require to be continually watched and reproved, or they will relapse into wickedness."[50]

Along with President Cannon's bold denunciation of evil, he exhibited a great deal of understanding and kindness in trying to help people overcome their weaknesses. Of one newly received "problem elder" from Zion, President Cannon wrote, "Before he arrived I had got an inkling of his drinking on the plains." In visiting with this young man, President Cannon told him that he would be of great value in the mission office for a few weeks and asked him to remain. Of course the mission president hoped that "if he were kept here for a few weeks, that his good resolutions would be strengthened and fortified by the influence that would be around him here."[51] But in spite of the president's efforts to help this missionary, his drinking continued and made him so ineffective in his field of labor that he had to be sent home. Under the weight of many problems such as these, President Cannon exclaimed in a letter to Brigham Young, "I have never in my life felt so much as I have of late how comparatively rare are the qualities of unswerving integrity and unyielding virtue among men."[52]

Because President Cannon had so much confidence and trust in the Lord, it was often difficult for him to sympathize with those who lacked the faith that their physical wants would be supplied and that their labors would be successful. Once he received a letter from two very discouraged elders in Holland saying they were out of money and did not know what to do. President Cannon sent them five pounds, but in a short time another letter came requesting more money, and "giving me a very gloomy and discouraging account of their position and prospects for doing anything, as the people did not like polygamy, etc. and thought them very bad men. The letter breathed such a hopeless spirit respecting the possibility of the Elders ever doing anything there and manifested such a lack of faith and such a disposition to magnify the difficulties that surrounded them that we (Brothers Amasa and Charles being here at the time) thought it would be wise to drop them a pointed letter in reply."[53] President Cannon concluded, "Since then their letters have been more cheerful."[54]

Much of the work of the ministry was done by British elders. Because those most qualified to serve in leadership capacities almost invariably emigrated to Zion, he frequently encountered problems: "We are calling out all the native help that is available; but there is a great dearth of suitable men for the ministry. I am trying to arrange matters, so that in case you should not think it wisdom to send any Elders here in the spring, the work will not suffer materially."[55]

In another letter President Cannon described the leadership problems many of these Elders had: "They are stereotyped in many respects, and ill-adapted to preside over a people such as the Latter-day Saints should be—a vigorous, growing people. They have good desires, and would like to see the work prosper, but they are in the way of its prosperity and the growth and development of the Saints. Of course there are exceptions, but this is the case with them generally."[56]

An excerpt from a letter to Heber C. Kimball gives further insight into the problems of some of the English Saints:

> There are many branches of the Church which contain members who have held standings there from the time the Gospel was first preached here until the present. They have seen and heard yourself and others of the first missionaries to this country preach and what they *think* they don't know would scarcely be worth learning. There are some who seem to act as though they thought it sufficient glory for them for one lifetime to have seen and heard Bro. Brigham and yourself preach. I am pleased to see the people value such privileges, for privileges indeed they are; but I would like to see them show by their fruits that they appreciate them in fact in their hearts and not in their words only.[57]

Some of the recently converted Saints in England were offended easily by instructions aimed at reforming them. In spite of the fact that the elders had good intentions, they at times experienced failures. Elder Joseph F. Smith, then serving a mission in England, wrote to President Cannon:

> One man took offence yesterday, because I wished those who were in the habit of drinking liquor to keep off the stand on the Sabbath, when their breath smelled; and in a few hours after meeting he sent President Shires a note, accompanied by his Elder's License and a penny for his *"Star,"* stating that he had burnt up his "hymnbook" and all other works that he had and would burn

the "Book of Mormon" as soon as he could "find it."[58]

Although a good deal of President Cannon's contact with the elders seems to have been in helping them solve problems, there were many encouraging aspects of the missionary work in Great Britain. He described to President Young the progress the Saints had made since his arrival: "We take pleasure in saying that there is a visible improvement in the feelings of the Saints, and there are accessions being made to the Church in about every place we have visited or heard from. We hope that this improvement and increase will become more and more apparent until the Spirit of Zion shall burn in every bosom, both among officers and members. We feel that it will."[59]

Many of the letters he received from missionaries in the field told of faith-promoting experiences and great success. Joseph Bull, the same elder who had been one of the printing missionaries in California and who was now laboring as a conference president in Leeds, wrote warmly of a certain Elder Lee, an old man, who was laboring under his direction with good results:

He is visiting the merchants at their stores, the clerks in their counting-houses and the people at their firesides. They are forcibly struck when they see a man at his advanced years, whose temples are adorned with silver hairs of age, who has left his home and traveled nearly 8,000 miles to preach the Gospel having neither purse nor scrip. They are astonished at the testimony he bears of the character and truth of our Prophet, Joseph Smith, and the fearful scenes of persecution which the Saints have had to pass through in the once United States of America, and this comes with greater weight when he can tell them that ofttimes he has tracked his family by the marks of blood on the snow-fields of the wild prairie. He feels well and rejoices in his labors.[60]

President Cannon's occasional conference with the elders not only gave them inspiration, but also encouraged him. Near the close of 1863 he was quite concerned over the large number of more experienced elders who would be returning to Zion in the spring, leaving the work to be done by "young Elders." "I determined to call them together and impart such instructions unto them as the Spirit may dictate."[61] Reporting to President Young the success of this week-long conference, he wrote:

> I was very much pleased at witnessing the great improvement there is apparent in the young Elders. Before the Conference took place I feared that the withdrawal of so many experienced Elders, as have been released to return in the Spring, would be seriously felt in the Mission, as the responsibilities would necessarily fall upon the young men in most instances; but since seeing and hearing them I feel convinced that those remaining will, with the help of the Lord, if they continue as they have begun, be made quite adequate to the labor devolving upon them. They are fast awakening to a sense of the responsibilities and importance of the Priesthood. During our meeting, union and love filled every heart, and our joy was too great for utterance.[62]

Twice during President Cannon's tenure as European Mission President, in the fall of 1862 and 1863, he toured the branches of the Church in Scandinavia, Holland, Switzerland and France.[63] On the first trip, Sister Cannon accompanied her husband. President Cannon had some reservations about taking her; he explained to Brigham Young the reason for his decision: "My wife's health has been so poor that I have thought it best to take her with me, with the hope that the trip would do her good. I debated in my own mind the propriety of this for awhile, as I had heard among other matters of gossip talked about one of my predecessors in the office the fact of his taking his wife with him on the continent urged or brought forward as proof of his extravagance; but I feel that if I were with you, to get your counsel, you would recommend it."[64]

On this same tour, President Cannon took along the promising young elder Joseph F. Smith, who at age twenty-three was already on his second mission for the Church, his first having been served at age fifteen in the Sandwich Islands. Their association on this mission in Europe served as a foundation for a lifetime of service in the kingdom together—fourteen years as fellow members of the Quorum of the Twelve, and eleven years as counselors together in the First Presidency of the Church.[65]

Although President Cannon could not understand the languages of the Saints in most of the countries he visited, he felt great love for these good people: "If I had leisure, I would willingly devote the time necessary to acquire their language in order that I might have the privilege of conversing with them and teaching them."[66] After visiting Scandinavia, Germany, Holland and Switzerland, and while en route to Paris, President Cannon wrote the feelings of his heart concerning the missionary work in these countries: "I feel satisfied that, with proper management and the blessing of the Lord, a good work can be accomplished there in Scandinavia and thousands yet be brought to rejoice in the truth. These have been my feelings in passing through Germany, Holland and Switzerland. Let liberty to preach the gospel be obtained by the servants of God, and thousands of the seed of Israel in these lands will . . . gladly obey the truth and rally around the standard which has been raised up."[67] He expressed the joy and gratitude the experiences of this European mission afforded him: "Since my departure from home I have enjoyed myself much in my labors; and my feelings of thankfulness to the Lord, I believe, have increased for his kindness to me in permitting me to live in this dispensation and to bear his holy Priesthood and to be closely associated with his chosen ministers, whose lives are being spent in bringing the children of men and the earth into that condition when His will shall be done upon the earth."[68]

One of the universal elements of nearly all missionary experiences during this time was bitter persecution by enemies of the restored gospel. "While the devil lives and has influence on the earth we need not expect, as Saints, to be permitted to indulge in ease," wrote President Cannon.[69] This persecution was so much a part of President Cannon's missionary experience that when there was a lull or a period of calm, he felt uneasy: "The quiet times that we have had of late and freedom from opposition here, I fear, caused many of the Priesthood and Saints to grow careless respecting their duties. I have been reminded very much of late of the expressions of the servants of God in the Book of Mormon respecting the slothfulness of the people and the ease with which the Adversary gains favor over them."[70]

It appears that the greatest amount of persecution came from apostates. Speaking of three such men who had joined forces, President Cannon asserted, "Apostates are not idle, but by the watchful diligence of the Elders they have been kept at bay and have been prevented from doing the sheep any harm." The particular strategy of these three apostates, "Briggs, Derry, Owen and company," was to stage public debates between Briggs, who posed as a dignitary of the Church, and Owen, who "brilliantly" made a fool of the "Mormon" official.[71] Writing to the Quorum of the Twelve, President Cannon referred to the efforts of other apostates, one of whom was "doing all in his power in public lectures of the most wicked and malignant character, to arouse a spirit of hatred and persecution against us. He has fully abandoned himself to the influence of the spirit of Satan, and indulges in every conceivable slander against us." But, he continued, "blind as many people are respecting the Truth, they are not so utterly destitute of reason and sense as to fail to perceive his inconsistency and falsehood, he having told them two stories both of which cannot possibly be true."[72]

In this same report to the Twelve, he exposed a gimmick that still another apostate was using. This man gave out handbills to President Cannon and other elders headed "One Hundred Guineas Reward" if they would meet him in public debate on a certain night and prove the doctrines of Mormonism to be true. President Cannon advised the elders "to refrain from noticing him in the least." On the night designated for this gathering, a large crowd congregated, but when no Mormons came to answer this man's challenge he was forced merely to deliver a lecture against the Church. This was not what the public came to see; his audience soon dispersed, leaving him alone and embarrassed.[73] "In Bath," President Cannon continued, "our people are much persecuted by a mob incited and headed by members of an anti-Mormon association which exists in that city. They have hired a hall quite close to that occupied by the Saints and are doing all in their power to break up our meetings there."[74]

In a letter to Heber C. Kimball, President Cannon related his firsthand experience with a similar mob:

No longer ago than last Sunday I attended a Conference at Bristol and our meeting house was surrounded during the three meetings which we held by a mob of the rabble, incited by an old apostate. They did all in their power to annoy us by pelting the people as they came in and went out, by hooting after them and yelling and pounding on the doors and window shutters. This apostate had been around the city all the previous day endeavoring to arouse a Spirit of persecution by declaring publicly that we were going to hold a Conference on the morrow, and that our designs were to entrap the people etc. etc. The only damage that was done by this outbreak was the breaking of a few panes of glass. Though there was such a horrid uproar outside of the house, inside all was peace and quietness. The Spirit of the Lord prevailed and we had an excellent conference.[75]

When the conference reconvened that evening, the mob had increased their noise so much "that it seemed almost impossible to make ourselves heard inside. But we besought the Lord to give us peace." Almost miraculously, policemen, who earlier that day had refused to assist the Saints, arrived at the meetinghouse and dispersed the disorderly crowd.[76]

In February of 1863, a missionary from the "New Organization of the Church" under "Young Joseph" [Reorganized Church] called on President Cannon and requested permission to preach to Latter-day Saint congregations in the Latter-day Saint meeting halls. When this permission was refused, he claimed it was unfair; the Mormons would not grant to him the same privileges they asked of sectarians. "I told him, that I would feel very differently were he an honest sectarian, who wished to set forth his views in sincerity; but he, himself, had once known the truth and had apostatized from it, and those who sent him were in the same condition, and I knew they were neither honest nor sincere. I knew their history well, and knew them to be base, bad men."[77]

The next Sunday, while President Cannon was preaching to the Saints, he noticed this same man sitting at the rear of the chapel. At the close of President Cannon's talk, the man arose and tried to gain control of the meeting. "I told him that if he did not sit down immediately, I should have him put in the charge of a police officer. At that he caved." Following the meeting, he somewhat apologetically told President Cannon that he had been merely laboring under the weight of his responsibility. "I replied that it was just as much responsibility as the devil had ever felt."[78]

The next day President Cannon sent a circular to all the presiding elders throughout the mission, putting them on their guard against this "wolf in sheep's clothing." He explained his philosophy in regard to debating the gospel with such characters: "My teachings to the Elders and Saints have been, not to descend from the dignity of their position to argue and hold controversy, neither with the Devil nor with those filled with his spirit. Nothing can be gained, I have told them, by reasoning with apostates, men who have known the Truth and denied it and forfeited the Spirit of the Lord and yielded themselves up to the spirit of the Evil One."[79]

This apostate did cause further trouble in the mission. At one meeting he refused to sit down, so the presiding elder dismissed the congregation, leaving him without an audience. Reflecting on the "New Organization," President Cannon lamented: "I regret greatly that many of the children or relatives of our beloved prophet should be connected in any way with such a crowd, many of whom sought and rejoiced over the death of their father. I feel convinced, however, that circumstances are being so overruled that they, or at least a portion of them, will yet have their eyes open to see their true position and where alone they can find the true friends of their father and family. It is my prayer that they may be thus enlightened."[80]

The "Manuscript History of the British Mission" records further instruments used to antagonize the Saints:

> Among other devices for "putting down Mormonism" an assort-
> ment of most melancholy caricatures, intended to represent
> prominent members of the Church, accompanied by horrid-look-
> ing "Bombastes Furioses," clad in skins and loaded with deadly
> weapons, exhibited as "destroying angels," are in circulation. But
> as these terrific images do not seem to intimidate us to such an
> extent as to stagnate our progress entirely, we are gravely informed
> that more than half the Saints perish on the way to Utah, whose
> loss, I suppose, is mainly attributable to the vast number of
> "bears, wolves, and snakes" with which the route is infested and
> whose fangs, they tell us, are venomous beyond conception![81]

President Cannon described some of the rumors used by oppo-
nents of the truth as "a lot of miserable stuff, which apostates
and others have a thousand times spewed forth, about murders
and so forth, committed under the sanction of the Priesthood in
the Valley."[82] An apostate who had served a mission for the
Church helped spread these accusations of "holy murder." President Cannon pointed out the inconsistency in this man's actions:
"The stories he now tells he says he knew while he was in Utah
and yet he came here on a mission and was here upwards of two
years ostensibly as a missionary to preach to the people the necessity of gathering to Utah!!"[83] This apostate sought to gain
publicity by declaring himself one who had been marked for
"Priesthood Assassination," and the person assigned to shed his
blood was none other than President George Q. Cannon. Seeking to draw a lesson from all of these persecutions, President
Cannon concluded: "The devil appears to be determined not to
let us forget that he still lives and is our implacable enemy."[84]

Affairs in the Nation's Capital

On Monday, May 5, 1862, while President Cannon was thoroughly engrossed in the spirit and labors of his mission, he received a telegram from President Brigham Young requesting him to sail immediately for Washington, D. C., to join William H. Hooper and work for the admission of Utah into the Union. The outbreak of hostilities between the northern and southern states presented what the people of Utah considered a favorable opportunity for their acceptance as a state. While many southern states were manifesting disloyalty by seceding from the Union, the Saints were demonstrating their support for the federal government by seeking admission. In January of that year, after Governor John W. Dawson had vetoed an act calling for a constitutional convention, the citizens of the territory exercised their right to popular government by calling mass meetings and electing sixty-six delegates to this proposed convention, which was held beginning January 20, 1862. These delegates drew up and recommended candidates for the following positions: for Governor, Brigham Young; for Lieutenant Governor, Heber C. Kimball; for member of congress, John M. Bernhisel. The name of the state was to be Deseret.[85]

A few days later the state constitution and these proposals were presented to the general public for a vote. An estimated 13,000 "free, white, male citizens of the United States over twenty-one years of age, and six months residents in the territory" voted unanimously in favor of the constitution and candidates.[86] During the same election, representatives were chosen for the "general assembly," which the constitution provided for. Learning the results of this election, Elder Cannon sent his congratulation to Governor Young:

The news contained in the two last letters has been very gratifying and cheering. The unanimity of feeling manifested by the people in their voting of the Constitution and the State officers, is pleasing to reflect upon. The recognition of yourself and Brother Heber as Governor and Lieutenant Governor will afford much pleasure to the Elders and Saints abroad, as I am sure it must do to the people at home. There is scarcely an individual in the Church that has not looked forward with anxious desire for the day to come when you should be president or governor in other matters beside what is termed spiritual.[87]

The newly elected legislature convened April 16, 1862 and chose various state officers, including William H. Hooper and George Q. Cannon as United States senators.[88] These senators were appointed to present the State Constitution and memorials for statehood to the Congress of the United States.[89] Ten days after the legislature convened, the *News* reported: "The Hon. W. H. Hooper, accompanied by Mr. C. W. West, took his departure on Saturday last for Washington City, in order to take his seat in the Senate of the Untied States to which he is one of the Senators elect from Deseret, in the event that the State shall be admitted into the Federation before the close of this session of Congress. His colleague, Mr. George Q. Cannon is expected to be in the Federal city on Mr. Hooper's arrival there, or within a short time thereafter."[90]

As soon as President Cannon received President Young's telegram, he began to make arrangements for his absence from the mission, calling Elder Jacob G. Bigler to take charge.[91] Arranging the affairs of the mission was somewhat complicated by the fact that both Presidents Lyman and Rich were released to return to Zion simultaneously. The three Apostles took passage for New York on the steamer *Kangaroo*, May 14, 1862.[92] It was not until he arrived in Washington, D. C., that President Cannon learned from Brother Hooper of his election as United States Senator. "I can say I was truly surprised. When I left Liverpool I could not think that I had been elected to this position. I feel truly grateful for the confidence my brethren have reposed in me." Having already spent a good deal of time in the halls of Congress, Elder Cannon was somewhat aware of a senator's role. Writing to President Young, he contrasted the worldly honor of being a senator with the greater privilege of being a member of Christ's Church:

> It is not a position which I myself should seek to fill; but which, being elected to, I should endeavor to magnify with an eye single to the Glory of God. The associations are not pleasant to me. The society of a humble Saint, enjoying the Spirit of his religion, would be far preferable to me than that of the whole U.S. Senate composed as it is of men who ignore and ridicule the power of the Holy Spirit and scoff at the revelations of Jesus. I would rather be a deacon in or only a member of The Church of Jesus Christ of Latter-day Saints than to be U.S. Senator, and even President of the United States, if such a thing were possible in my case, without the deaconship or the membership. These have ever been my feelings, and I trust that whatever the glitter or the pomp of worldly power I may be thrown in contact with, they ever may be [my feelings]. You will pardon this brief expression of my feelings at this time; I felt to give them and have done so.[93]

The circumstances surrounding the mission assigned Brothers Hooper and Cannon were anomalous. The two titular senators were representing a nonexistent state and were seeking to be heard by an assembly in which they had no legal status. Before their case came up, the senators laid all the groundwork possible to attain statehood, including an interview with President Abraham Lincoln. In a letter to Amasa M. Lyman, Senator Cannon reported their activities and prospects for success:

> Since our arrival here (June 7th) we have been very busy. We have seen and had conversations with the President, Secretary of State, nearly every Senator and a large number of the members of the House of Representatives. We have spared no pains in seeking interviews and in laying our business and the wants of our people before them. We have been treated with courtesy and respect by all with whom we have met, excepting Garrett Davis, Senator from Kentucky; he told us point blank, and very rudely, that he should oppose our admission and, when we attempted to explain matters to him, cut us short and said there was no use in prolonging the interview. We have found a better, kinder feeling among public men than I ever witnessed before, and many say that they cannot see any reason why we should not be admitted. We may not be admitted; how this will be I cannot say.[94]

In early January, the Constitution and memorials for admission to the union were presented to the House by Delegate Bernhisel, and the following day they were presented to the Senate by the vice president. In both houses the matter was referred to committees on territories, where, for all practical purposes, it died. For several years polygamy and slavery had been commonly referred to as the "twin relics of barbarism," a phrase popularized by Stephen A. Douglas.[95] With the nation involved in full-scale war against one of these "relics," there was little likelihood that they would be willing to accept the other. The *Deseret News* gave the following as a reason for the tabling of the statehood question: "Congress, during its last session was heavily burdened with duties pertaining to the conduct of the war then and still being prosecuted for the restoration of the Union, and, so far as I have been advised, took no action on our petition."[96]

To make matters worse, the two senators witnessed the passage of the first of a number of anti-polygamy laws; on July 8, 1862, the president signed the Morrill Act or Anti-Bigamy Law of 1862. Although the efforts toward statehood had once again been foiled, the people of Utah were still willing to cast their lot with the North: "Utah provoked much respect from members of Congress over her conduct at that moment, when it was thought by no inconsiderable portion of the world that the issues of war would be won by the South."[97] When Congress adjourned, President Cannon returned to England, arriving there July 26, 1862.[98] When President Young commended him for his efforts in the Senate, President Cannon expressed his faith that the Lord's will would be done:

I am gratified that our labors at Washington have been satisfactory to yourself and our constituents, and in learning that the non-admission of our State into the family has not been attributed (which we felt would not be) to any lack of diligence or faithfulness upon our part to the interest of Deseret. It is delightful to know that there is a people upon the earth who have such confidence in their God, in his mercy and goodness, that they are not afraid, after they have done that which they could, to trust him with the results in all cases.[99]

Back to England

In England, George Q. Cannon resumed the presidency of the European Mission. At age thirty-six, with the staggering responsibility of the entire mission resting on his shoulders, Elder George Q. Cannon felt a great yearning for the fellow members of his quorum. To President Brigham Young he wrote: "Our constant prayers are that your life and the lives of the brethren may be preserved and that our enemies may have no power to cause you one moment's annoyance or uneasiness. I speak the feelings of all the Elders, I believe, when I say, that if there were any trouble at home we would feel exceedingly anxious to be with you. I have been often with you, of late, in my dreams."[100]

To Elder Lyman, he pined, "I scarcely thought when you left that I would miss yourself and brother Charles as much as I have done, though I dreaded your departure very much."[101] And to Elder Heber C. Kimball he wrote: "Being off so far from my brethren, and so few being here comparatively speaking, upon whom I can lean, makes one feel to strengthen the bonds, if possible, which connect one with my brethren at home in Zion, and cling closer to them. This feeling has increased very much since the departure of Bros. Amasa and Charles. I did not feel the responsibility that rested upon me to so great an extent then as I do at the present; at that time it was divided, and I felt that I was not alone."[102]

It added to his loneliness when he decided to send Elizabeth home. This decision was doubtless a difficult one to make, but her health was impaired, "the climate not agreeing with her";[103] and the threat of war between Britain and the United States was increasing. Thus, for reasons of health and safety, he felt that Elizabeth should return. Five months after arriving in England, she had given birth to their first daughter, Georgiana Hoagland Cannon, and on May 21, 1863, just one month before her departure for America, another son, George Hoagland Cannon, was born to them. The Cannons also adopted a ten-year-old girl, Rosina Matthews Cannon, while in England.[104]

Returning to America with three children was a precarious

undertaking for Sister Cannon in her poor health, and it doubtless would not have been attempted if the possibility of greater
danger had not been threatening. President Cannon's decision to
send his family may have been influenced by the fact that one of
his most trusted missionaries, Joseph F. Smith, was returning to
Zion at that time.[105] At Liverpool Elder Smith, the little family,
and several other returning missionaries embarked on the
steamship *City of Washington* on June 24, 1863. This was the last
time George Q. Cannon ever saw Georgiana and George alive,
for his little daughter died on the plains before reaching the valley, and his newborn son passed away shortly after arriving
home. Elizabeth was so stricken with the loss of Georgiana that,
as with the death of her first child, she would not allow her
daughter to be buried away from the valley. A small airtight casket was fashioned out of the butter churn, and in it Georgiana's
body was carried to the Valley for burial.[106] The next sixteen
months until President Cannon was reunited with his loved ones
in the valley must have been sad ones indeed for the lonely and
grieving young mission president.

The Gathering to Zion Continues

Besides the publishing and the missionary work, President
Cannon was also responsible for sending faithful Saints to gather
to Zion. In June, September, and October of 1840, Elder
Brigham Young had arranged for the first three emigrant vessels,
carrying a total of three hundred Saints to Nauvoo. During the
next twenty years an average of nearly a thousand Saints per year
gathered from England, and thousands more came from other
countries.[107] In the early 1850s the Perpetual Emigration Fund
began to provide means for some eager converts to emigrate, but

it could not fulfill this desire for all of them. President Young's counsel, however, was to come to Zion with or without help from the fund: "Let all the Saints, who can, gather up for Zion and come while the way is open before them; let the poor also come whether they receive aid or not from the [P. E.] Fund; let them come on foot with handcarts or wheelbarrows. Let them gird up their loins and walk through, and nothing shall hinder or stay them."[108] The difficult decision of who would receive aid from the fund was made by the district presidents: "In the selection of persons to be emigrated by these donations, regard is had first to the integrity and moral worth, second to occupation. The selection is made largely by the conference [district] presidents who should be able to judge."[109]

Thousands of these newcomers to Zion brought with them well-developed skills and trades that were much needed in the founding of the mountain kingdom. The British Manuscript History contains almost endless lists of emigrants' names followed by their trades. Some of the dozens listed are:

cord winder	hair dresser	embroiderer	surveyor
basket maker	upholsterer	general dealer	milkman
gun smith	plate layer	miller	joiner
boot closer	tallow candler	last maker	brush maker
carriage maker	brick maker	lamb keeper	stevedore
book binder	undertaker	saddler	brewer
weaver	sawyer	general servant	gardener
school master	iron founder	surgeon	coppersmith
butcher	glass blower	fisherman	bone cutter
engineer	roper	porter	dyer
watchmaker	stone cutter	paper hanger	laborer
glass cutter	paper maker	tin man	printer
baker	silk twister	pilot	barman
dredger	smith	comb maker	
screw maker	knitter	puddler	
hatter	engine driver	file hardener	
coachman	stone mason	cooper	

The *Millennial Star* disseminated information about emigration to the widely scattered Saints:

> Emigration—As the season of emigration is again close at hand, we wish to draw attention of the Saints to the subject. We do not expect to give, in a single article, all that we may have to publish in relation to this matter; but shall write, from time to time, such counsel and items of information as we may deem expedient. The first step to be taken by the Saints, who intend emigrating the coming season, is to send up to this office their names, orders, and deposits. This should be attended to without delay, to enable us to make timely arrangements in the other side of the water for the purchase of the outfit needed for the Plains.[111]

From sixty to ninety days before the sailing date, notices like the following would appear:

> NOTICE TO INTENDING EMIGRANTS—We beg to inform the Saints intending to emigrate, that we are now prepared to receive their applications for berths. Every application should be accompanied by the name, age, occupation, country where born, and a one pound deposit for each one named. Passengers must furnish their own beds and bedding, their cooking utensils, provision boxes. . . .[112]

The business experience that Elder Cannon had gained in arranging for outfits and supplies for emigration from the frontier to the valley during his mission in the East served him well as the basis for the acumen he developed in England in dealing with shipping companies. The volume of business conducted by President Cannon was comparable in the eyes of these companies to that done by an entire nation in a given period of time.

Occasionally, even railroad travel for Saints gathering to the port of embarkation was obtained at reduced rates because of the large numbers.[113] In making these large business transactions with thousands of dollars of Church money involved, President Cannon constantly besought and received the Lord's help. In April 1864, he reported to President Young: "So far I have been extremely fortunate and blessed of the Lord in chartering. The 'Monarch of the Sea' is now worth £ 400 or £ 500 more than I succeeded in obtaining her for. For two weeks past, passages to New York have ranged from £ 5 to £ 5, 10 per head. . . . I am letting the Saints have their tickets for £ 4, 5."[114]

A month later, he told of making a deal with the captain of the *General M'Clellan*. In speaking with the captain, President Cannon explained the holy purpose for which the vessel was being chartered and succeeded in closing the contract at eight shillings a head. The captain later wanted to rescind the agreement, but President Cannon knew a blessing from the Lord when he saw one:

I saw him this morning and closed the charter. He offered me £ 30 down to let him off, and said he could get 5 shillings more per head than he had proposed to let me have her at. . . . In alluding to the offer which he had made, he seemed to be much vexed with himself, and said that his feelings had entirely overpowered his judgment. I could account for this, though I did not tell him so, for brothers James Townsend, Jesse N. Smith, your son John W. and myself, together with the brethren in the office, had been praying unitedly and exercising our faith that we might get the vessel on such terms as would enable the Saints to emigrate, and that the hearts of those that had the power might be softened so that we might gain our point.[115]

On some occasions it seemed the Lord provided vessels for Elder Cannon when none were available to professional shipping agents. "I feel that I have been exceedingly blessed under the circumstances, as many offices in town are compelled to refund the people their money, it being out of their power to furnish them passages."[116] The scarcity of ships was caused by problems relating to the American Civil War, problems that caused President Cannon and the waiting Saints a great deal of anxiety. There was a delicate peace being maintained between England and the United States, but the possibility of war threatened. President Cannon wrote to Brigham Young: "The Government is making active preparations for war. Great activity prevails in all the navy yards of this country, and the military are being prepared as rapidly as possible. It is reported that two of Cunard's steamships, besides other steamers, have been chartered for the purpose of taking troops to Canada."[117]

He further voiced his concern for the emigration: "If war should break out, it will seriously interfere with our emigration. Even as it is, the prospect does not look promising for obtaining ships at low rates."[118] In the fall of that year, the rebel steamship *Nashville* captured and destroyed the *Harvey Binch,* a merchant vessel from New York. In consequence of this, President Cannon wrote: "Masters of American vessels in this port are trembling in their shoes at the thought of going to sea with such ugly customers afloat on their path as these rebel steamships. Since this news has reached here war risks on all vessels bearing the American flag have increased enormously."[119] As a result of this threat, the emigration of the Saints took place on vessels bearing the English flag.[120] This precarious peace caused a great deal of fear that something would happen to isolate the English Saints from Zion. Elder Cannon hoped the emigration would

not be interrupted: "If it be the Lord's will we would like to see
the way kept open until the honest and the meek in these lands
are gathered out."[121] He expressed his faith and trust that the
Lord was still at the helm and would not forsake his people: "I
feel, however, that all is right; the Lord knows what is best, and
he will consummate his purposes, and if we only do our duty
the promised salvation will not be wanting. Whatever the result
of this affair may be, I feel that it will all be overruled for the
Lord's work and people."[122]

The Civil War in America and the possibility of war with
England were not the only conflicts that made President Cannon's
job as emigration agent difficult. Near the close of 1861 he wrote
of the problems encountered by native Danish missionaries:

> According to present appearances Germany and Denmark are
> likely to come to blows over the Schleswig Holstein difficulty. In
> anticipation of war, Denmark is bringing her army up to its max-
> imum strength. Many of our native missionaries are being drafted
> into the army and they are considerably excited over the matter. A
> few of the Saints, young men, who have means and who are liable
> to the draft are leaving for this country and are pushing on from
> here to the States. It seems as though it will not be long before
> those who are in Europe who wish to escape the dreadful neces-
> sity of having to take the sword to fight against their neighbors
> will also have to flee to Zion.[123]

A few weeks later, this conflict did erupt. Before this, emigrating
Scandinavian Saints had traveled to Germany and had embarked
from Hamburg,[124] but this war, President Cannon said, "has
made the adoption of a new route necessary as all regular travel
between Denmark and Germany has ceased."[125]

Another constant danger to the safety of the emigrants was

the unpredictable weather. "For the past two or three weeks the weather has been very trying to the health and few are free from the ill effects of the change. The coast has been visited by several very severe gales, and shipping has experienced more disasters, and there has been a greater loss of life, than has been experienced here for several years."[126] Nearly every company of Mormon emigrants buried one or two of their number at sea, but on one particular voyage a great tragedy occurred that brought President Cannon deep sorrow. Writing to President Young of this calamitous voyage, he said:

> I have been much saddened by hearing of the number of deaths which occurred among the children of the Saints on the "Monarch of the Sea" in her voyage to New York. There were forty-five deaths, and with one or two exceptions, all children under eight years of age. Though there were British Saints on board, there were no deaths among their children from sickness— the only child which they lost being killed by an accident. The doctor who accompanied the ship, and who crossed with a company of our people once before, attributes great mortality among the Scandinavian children . . . to their objection to giving their children air, muffling them up in numberless garments. I think however that the difference between the health of their children and the English may be found in their having made a long journey before being embarked on the "Monarch of the Sea" and having been subjected to more or less exposure. Every care was taken, in examining the passengers, to detect all symptoms of sickness, and a number of persons who gave signs of fever were brought on shore and kept by me until the next ship sailed.[127]

But in spite of these and many other difficulties, thousands of determined Latter-day Saints set sail for America under President Cannon's able direction. In fact, the number of emigrants increased each year except 1864. Indications of these numbers can be traced in letters Elder Cannon wrote to President Brigham Young. A few weeks after his arrival in England, he reported the number of baptisms and emigrants for 1860: "These figures give a total of 4,518 for the missions during the year just ended. There having been an emigration of about 2,000 leaves an increase over and above the emigration of 2,500 and upwards."[128] During 1861, the number of emigrants increased by about 850, making the total near 2,850.[129] Included in this number were a few Saints from far away South Africa: "A small company of Saints, numbering about twenty-two, are now here from the Cape of Good Hope, waiting to proceed to Florence with the company per *Underwriter*."[130]

The year 1862 saw the emigration jump another 650. This report to President Young gives insight into the busy schedule of Brother Cannon's emigration season: "We are very busy at the present having sent off a vessel last week ("John J. Boyd") with 702 souls aboard, and are now ticketing etc. for the "Manchester" which sails on Monday, the 5th, with about 400 on board. The 'Wm. Tapscott' is chartered to sail on the 13th inst. with between 800 and 900 souls. From Hamburg four ships have already sailed, carrying in the aggregate about 1,556 souls of the Scandinavian Saints. Altogether our emigration will number upwards of 3,500 souls from Europe this season."[131]

At the close of the emigration season in 1863, Elder Cannon sent this report: "On the 30th day of May the ship 'Cynosure' sailed, having on board 776 souls of the Saints, and on the 4th inst. the 'Amazon' sailed from London, having on board 895 souls making a total of 3650 souls who have left England en route for Zion this spring."[132] The minutes of a general conference held in Birmingham record, "There have been a little over ten thousand Saints who have emigrated from Europe during the past three years."[133]

It appears that in 1864 the number of emigrants may have been down slightly: "The nearest estimate that I can make of the probable number of saints who will emigrate this season from Europe, from all the information there is before me, is about 2,200 from Great Britain etc., and about 1,100 from Scandinavia, making a total of about 3,300. These numbers, so far as Great Britain is concerned, are, if anything, I think, below what the probable actual emigration will be, should every thing move off as favorable as the Saints hope and pray will be the case."[134]

The results of this bounteous emigration were not only gratifying to President Cannon, but, he recorded, "it is cheering to the Elders to see so many breaking loose from Babylon and misery and it has the effect to stir the Saints up to diligence."[135] When the Saints arrived on the eastern seaboard of America, they were met by agents with the same assignment Elder Cannon had filled during his mission to the East, who forwarded them on to Florence, Nebraska, at the frontier. Here, if they had sufficient funds, they purchased outfits and supplies and made their way to the Valley. But, as was more often the case, the poorer Saints were met by Church teams that conveyed them to their new home. Although there were Church agents in Florence to take care of these arrangements, Elder Cannon was still somewhat involved in this aspect of their journey. To President Young he wrote concerning Saints he had forwarded to the frontier the first season, "The news that all the poor who had gone to Florence from the States and this country had been taken through was almost more than I dared expect."[136] Then, anticipating the next spring's emigration, he asked, "If there should be no obstacle in the way to prevent the Saints from reaching the frontier this ensuing spring what will be the prospects of teams coming down as they did last spring to assist the poor and what will be the probable number that can be taken?"[137]

A letter from Elder Orson Pratt indicates the volume of this Church team operation: "Our latest advices from Utah inform us that 200 wagons, with four yoke of oxen each, and some loose cattle, left for the frontiers on the 21st of April, bringing with them about 150,000 lbs. of flour, to be deposited at different points east of the South Pass, for the benefit of our emigration. All things are in a flourishing condition in our Territory."[138]

A letter from one of the recipients of this noble Church team service described some of the hardships the trains encountered coming east to Florence: "A few companies of the Church train have arrived. . . . They report a very wet time—sometimes rolling in mud up to the hubs of the wheels, and crossing bottoms with the cattle at times swimming, and the water running in the wagon beds enough to wet everything; but mountain boys have learned to a great extent to cope with the elements, and by the blessing of God and their own exertions, have reached us in safety."[139]

One of these "mountain boys," Joseph W. Young, the originator of "oxteamology," complained to President Cannon about the European emigrants: "I . . . speak of those who leave Europe expecting to be picked up at Florence by Church teams. Many . . . bring with them large amounts of fine clothing and can outshine any of the wives or daughters of those who furnish teams and means to bring them here."[140] Brother Young went on to conjecture that the emigrating Saints were spending on unnecessary items the money they saved by not having to buy an outfit, which only added to the weight the teams had to pull through the mountains. The excess was not entirely the fault of the emigrants—they brought some of this luggage because their relatives and friends in the Valley wrote letters advising them to buy goods that were cheaper in England and the States; Brother Young described them as saying, "Bring this, bring that, you can buy it so cheap there, and here it is very dear." His reply was: "Nonsense. I say to the Saints, bring yourselves, with strong hands and willing hearts, and you are rich. But do not accumulate a great debt upon yourselves by bringing a great amount of fine dresses, ribbons and gewgaws." Demonstrating his knowledge of "oxteamology," Joseph Young gave his reasons for condemning this practice: "Now, where is the advantage in freighting a hundred pounds more than a team ought to take, making thereby fifteen or twenty dollars and using up a yoke of cattle worth a hundred dollars in doing so."[141]

The team drivers were not the only ones to complain about the weight of the Saints' baggage. The sea captains in the English ports before they even set sail noticed the added weight in their ships: "Mormon companies were known for their heavy luggage. Mechanics and other craftsmen who made up a large percentage of the emigrants brought all available tools which caused some of the ships captains to complain that their vessels lay at least an inch lower in the water."[142] But if the captains had this complaint about their Mormon passengers, it appears that they had few others. Before embarking, President Cannon organized the Saints into wards presided over by returning missionaries. Each ward had a section of deck assigned to them to keep clean.[143] "There were school classes for children and organized lectures for adults. Times were set for community prayers and services. At well-regulated hours the Saints turned out to disinfect their quarters, use the galley in turn, and take their health in the bracing sea air on deck."[144]

President Cannon personally supervised this organization on

each departing vessel. Naomi Dowden, a passenger on one of the emigrant ships, recorded in her journal, "George Q. Cannon gave the departing Saints instructions and appointed officers for the company."[145] Another passenger, John Durrant, recorded, "The tugboat tugged us out to anchor and Brother George Q. Cannon . . . came out to us and organized our brethren for the trip, and preached to us about being patient with one another and trying to help one another."[146] Elder Cannon expressed the need for these counseling sessions:

> We are desirous at all times to inform the Saints correctly on all matters which may have bearing on their salvation, temporally or spiritually. We find it necessary sometimes to teach the Saints on simple matters. . . . But as the Saints, though many of them long in the Church, are quite inexperienced, we feel to talk kindly to them and give them such instructions as may benefit them, even though they may be, as it were, the first principles.[147]

Sometimes, however, this counsel went beyond "the first principles." In one emigrant's journal, he recalled President Cannon coming on board the ship just prior to its departure and "advising many young couples to get married since the vessel was overcrowded and it would make traveling more comfortable for all."[148]

The happiness the Saints radiated was contagious—as were their spirituality and their testimony of the gospel: "On board ship there was a good band that discoursed lively music and dancing was indulged in. Meetings were held on the ship which the ship's captain and officers attended."[149] It was not uncommon for members of the crews or even the officers of the ships to be converted and baptized during these voyages, and on at least two occasions, nearly the whole crew joined the Church.[150]

A striking example of the influence that the Saints exerted upon gentile sailors occurred a few years earlier:

> The Saints without exception have enjoyed a great amount of the spirit of God. . . . These things and the good conduct of the Saints, have had a happy result in bringing many to a knowledge of the truth. And I am now glad to inform you that we have baptized all on board except three persons. We can number the Captain, first and second mates, with eighteen of the crew most of whom intend going right through to the Valley. The carpenter and eight of the seamen are Swedish, German and Dutch. There are two negroes and others from Otaheite, etc. Many of them have already testified to the truth of this work, and are rejoicing in anticipation of building up Zion. . . . The number baptized in all is forty-eight since we left our native shores.[151]

Liverpool was the port of embarkation for nearly all the ships chartered by the Mormons. The first ship to be sent from another English port was the *Amazon*, which sailed from London. Elder Cannon wrote, "I did not know when I chartered the 'Amazon', that I was fulfilling a prediction of Brother Kelsey's uttered some years ago in London, to the effect that a ship or ships would yet leave that port laden with Saints."[152] Mormon emigration had become well known during the past twenty-three years, and the departure of a vessel from London attracted a great deal of attention:

> The "Amazon" is the finest vessel I have sent out this season, and everything connected with her departure (with the exception of being a few days later than I could have wished) passed off in a most satisfactory manner. The company as a whole were so much superior in appearance to the ordinary emigrants as to excite

general admiration. The Government Officers, and others who visited the ship out of curiosity, of whom there were a great number, clergymen, public men etc., were loud in their praise of their appearance. I received many compliments on these points.[153]

As a result of one visitor's observations, Mormon emigration received a great deal of favorable publicity. This visitor was none other than the famous English writer Charles Dickens. In reporting this visit to President Brigham Young, Elder Cannon said: "Mr. Charles Dickens, the novelist, spent several hours on board on the day when the people passed the Government Inspectors. He appeared to be very much pleased with the people and had a great many questions to ask of me, appearing to be much interested in us and free from prejudice."[154]

Elder Cannon's modest description of Charles Dickens's visit does not nearly convey the importance that the novelist himself placed on his encounter with the Saints. He paints a warm and vivid picture of his visit, declaring that the degree of prejudice he had entertained before coming on board was completely obliterated. Bearing the symbolic name of Mr. "Uncommercial Traveler" and representing a fictitious company which he called "The Firm of Human Interest Brothers," Dickens came aboard the emigrant ship "to see what eight hundred Latter-day Saints were like, and I found them (to the rout and overthrow of all my expectations) like what I now describe with scrupulous exactness."[155] Dickens readily admitted that he came on board the Latter-day Saint vessel "to bear testimony against them if they deserved it, as I fully believed they would." But, he continued, "to my great astonishment, they did not deserve it; and my predispositions and tendencies must not affect me as an honest witness."[156] This "honest witness" gave a very thorough, almost dramatic, description of the fine appearance and decorum of the Saints:

> Nobody is in an ill-temper, nobody is the worse for drink, no-body swears an oath or uses a coarse word, nobody appears de-pressed, nobody is weeping. . . . Now I have seen emigrant ships before this day in June. And these people are so strikingly differ-ent from all other people in like circumstances whom I have ever seen, that I wonder aloud, "What would a stranger suppose these emigrants to be!"[157]

In speaking with the ship's captain, Dickens learned of the marvelous organization that Brother Cannon had effected on board. The captain said: "The most of these came aboard yes-terday evening. They came from various parts of England in small parties that had never seen one another before. Yet they had not been a couple of hours on board, when they established their own police, made their own regulations, and set their own watches at all the hatchways. Before nine o'clock the ship was as orderly and as quiet as a man-of-war."[158]

The captain asked "Uncommercial" what he would have supposed these people to be had he not known they were Mor-mons. "I should have said they were in their degree, the pick and flower of England." "So should I," the captain agreed.[159] Mr. Dickens even went so far as to describe George Q. Cannon in his account, leaving for posterity one of the most vivid descriptions of him:

> The Mormon Agent who had been active in getting them to-gether, and in making the contract with my friends the owners of the ship to take them as far as New York on their way to the Great Salt Lake, was pointed out to me. A compactly-made

handsome man in black, rather short, with rich-brown hair and beard, and clear bright eyes. From his speech, I should set him as American. Probably, a man who had "knocked about the world" pretty much. A man with a frank open manner, and unshrinking look; withal a man of great quickness.[160]

Apparently President Cannon greeted the famous man with as much calmness as he had used in reporting his visit to President Young, for Dickens said, "I believe he was wholly ignorant of my Uncommercial importance."[161] President Cannon also managed to astonish "Uncommercial" with another very suave comment. Dickens observed to President Cannon, "Indeed, I think it would be difficult to find eight hundred people together anywhere else, and find so much beauty and so much strength and capacity for work among them." Instead of being flustered by so great a compliment, President Cannon told Dickens where he could find other such groups:. "The Mormon Agent (not looking about, but looking steadily at Uncommercial)" replied, "We sent out about a thousand more, yes'day from Liverpool."[162] Charles Dickens left the vessel impressed, and puzzled over what great spirit could have produced such a group: "I went over the Amazon's side, feeling it impossible to deny that, so far, some remarkable influence had produced a remarkable result, which better-known influences have often missed."[163] Mr. Dickens concluded his article on the Mormons with a footnote in which he quoted a certain Lord Houghton, who, nine years earlier, had also found that the Mormon emigration was above reproach:

The Select Committee of the House of Commons on emigrant ships for 1854 summoned the Mormon agent and passenger-broker before it, and came to the conclusion that no ships under the provisions of the "Passenger Act" could be depended upon for comfort and security in the same degree as those under his administration. The Mormon ship is a Family under strong and accepted discipline, with every provision for comfort, decorum, and internal peace.[164]

The power that organized hundreds of people into a "Family" within hours and that "produced a remarkable result, which better-known influences have often missed," was the restored priesthood, to which authority the devoted Saints willingly submitted.

Early in June 1863, the *Amazon* set sail. One of its passengers recorded the occurrence of an event that happened from time to time aboard the emigrant ships, the birth of a child. The poor little girl, by dint of her birthplace, was the victim of a practice not uncommon in those days—she was named after the ship: "On the evening of the 9th we hove up anchor and slipped round the corner of the island, under the influence of a gentle breeze, having received an addition to our company, in the shape of a fine girl born to brother and sister Harris, from Stratford, on the morning of the 7th, which was blessed under the name of Amazon Seaborn Harris."[165]

The Latter-day Saints continued to impress their captain favorably throughout the entire journey, and when he returned to England he sought out President Cannon with the hope of carrying another shipload of Saints to America: "The 'Amazon', which took out the company of Saints from London, has returned, and the Captain expresses his great satisfaction, and he says that if I do not want to ship from London that he will come around to Liverpool. He thinks he will be ready to sail about the middle of April. I should be pleased to have the 'Amazon', if we can obtain her upon suitable terms, as she is a really splendid vessel, and Captain Hovery, a gentlemanly, energetic man."[166]

But alas, before she could be chartered again, a letter to President Young five weeks later told the sad conclusion to the *Amazon* story: "The ship 'Amazon' about which I wrote you in a former letter, has since been entirely destroyed by fire. She caught fire soon after starting from London and while close to the Coast."[167]

During his tenure as mission president, George Q. Cannon arranged passage for more than 13,000 European Saints and saw a larger number than that baptized who did not emigrate during his presidency.[168] In his homecoming address in Salt Lake City, he compared the work of gathering modern Israel to Moses' gathering of ancient Israel:

> To my mind, the great work in which we are engaged is far greater than the work that was performed by Moses. I reverence the work Moses performed; I look upon it as a great work, but this work of the last days—the gathering of the Saints together from the various nations is a far more stupendous work, to my mind, than the gathering of Israel from Egypt to the land of Canaan.[169]

Home to Zion at Last

Notwithstanding President Cannon's many joys and successes in England, his heart was never far from his family in Zion. Surely it must have been difficult for Elder Cannon to send so many thousands of eager Saints to the Valley and to watch dozens of happy missionaries return to their friends and loved ones and yet he himself have to remain behind. He was not called to England for any specific length of time, and so he awaited President Young's decision to call him home. In corresponding with the prophet on this subject, he showed his great loyalty to Brigham Young and the gospel cause: "Upon this point I still feel as I ever have felt, to be in your hands like clay in the hands of the potter, and to take pleasure in returning or in remaining just as you shall dictate."[170] President Young's summons finally came in the spring of 1864. President Cannon's duties in England detained him until the end of summer. In responding to President Young's call to return, he wrote,

> For my own part, I have ever been thankful to the Lord for his kindness to me in permitting me to be his servant, and in calling me to go forth as one of his messengers to the nations; but I believe I am just as thankful now to have the privilege of returning to once more enjoy your and the brethren's and Saints' society in Zion as I ever have been to go away.[171]

The *Millennial Star* carried this notice in President Cannon's last editorial, entitled "Valedictory":

> In the kind providence of our Heavenly Father, after a mission of three years and eight months in these lands, making an absence from home of close upon four years, I have had the privilege granted unto me of returning home to Zion. It is with deep feeling that I make this announcement at the present time to the Elders and Saints through the columns of the "Star." Though I have always been satisfied to labor wherever the Lord has seen fit through his servants to direct, I have, nevertheless, yearned for the time to come when I could return with His approval, and the good feelings and confidence of His servants, and a consciousness within myself of having done my duty to enjoy the society of my brethren and the rest of the people of God in the home which he has provided for them in the midst of the mountains. That time has at length arrived.[172]

The remainder of this editorial was written with great emotion.

He expressed his gratitude to the English Saints and elders, whom he had grown to love:

> I cannot say Farewell to you, my brethren and sisters, without thanking you for the faith you have exercised in my behalf and for the many acts of kindness which I . . . have received at your hands, and for the willingness which you have generally manifested to give heed to the teachings and counsels which have been imparted unto you.[173]

He left them this advice: "My parting exhortation to you is, Seek constantly in mighty faith, for the Spirit of God to be increased upon you." He bore to them this solemn witness: "My last testimony to you, . . . is the same as it has ever been, that in taking this course, . . . you can obtain eternal salvation, happiness and exaltation." The editorial concluded with this powerful blessing, which President Cannon pronounced on the European Saints:

> May the blessing of God rest down upon you, one and all, and may the way be opened before every faithful soul—man, woman, and child—to gather up to Zion; and I bless you, and all the honest-in-heart, in the name of Jesus and by the authority which he has given me, that you . . . may be preserved from every calamity and escape the destructions which will come upon this nation and the other nations of Babylon, even so, Amen.[174]

The same issue of the *Star* carried this loving farewell from the European Saints:

> We feel that we only respond [with] the heartfelt emotions of thousands when we say God bless you, Brother Cannon; and to the happy consciousness of the faithful and honest performance

of arduous and responsible duties, may there be speedily added, in sweet solace and great enjoyment, the associations of family and friends in our Mountain Home.[175]

Brother Cannon hoped to arrive in Utah in time for the October Conference, but was detained in the East for several weeks by an Indian War that he described in a letter to President Daniel Wells and Brigham Young, Jr., who replaced him as the presidents of the European Mission: "We wrote our last to you on the 7th instant. . . . After mailing that letter we went down to Mr. Holladay's office and learned from him, to our very great surprise . . . that the Stage . . . would not be running again for a week or fortnight. The Sioux, Arapahoe, and Crow Indians had made a combined descent on the trains running to Santa Fe, or New Mexico, Colorado and Utah Territories, attacking settlements, mail stations, and Government and emigrant trains, killing great numbers of men, women and children, running off stock and creating great terror by the boldness of their movements."[176]

President Cannon's desire to reach home was so strong that he started across the plains even before it was considered safe to travel. "But," he said, "we were preserved from every danger, though we felt throughout the entire journey that it was necessary to exercise all the faith we could muster."[177] George Q. Cannon arrived in the Valley early in October, shortly after general conference. Of all his homecomings, this was the sweetest. To his successors in England he wrote:

You can imagine, far better than I can describe, my feelings upon reaching home and meeting with . . . my family and friends. I never felt better in returning home than I have done this time. My feelings were peculiar, and for weeks, I felt it would be a relief for me to get off into a corner and weep for joy.[178]

As a boy coming from Liverpool to Zion, he had dreamed of being a standard bearer of the gospel. Now, as a man, he again came from Liverpool to Zion, having nobly fulfilled his cherished boyhood dream.

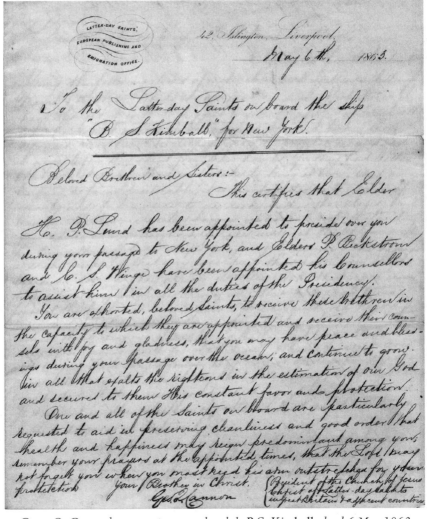

George Q. Cannon letter to emigrants on board the B.S. Kimball, *dated 6 May 1863*

CHAPTER 8

Conclusion

GEORGE Q. CANNON'S RETURN from Great Britain took place almost fifteen years to the day from that October morning when as a young man of twenty-two, responding to the call of the Church, he had set out on horseback for California on his first mission. During these fifteen years, Elder Cannon was away from home for fourteen years and three months, serving five consecutive missions for the Church. His return from England in 1864 concluded the missionary period of his life. He was thirty-seven years old. He would live another thirty-seven years, rendering more valiant service to the kingdom of God in Zion as a

George Q. Cannon portrait
from the St. George Temple

counselor to Presidents Brigham Young, John Taylor, Wilford
Woodruff, and Lorenzo Snow, until his death, April 12, 1901,
at the age of seventy-four. A letter he wrote to President Young
from Liverpool, on November 12, 1862, expresses the spirit in
which his years of missionary service were performed and his
resolution to carry this spirit with him throughout his life:

> My prayer to the Lord is, that as long as I live upon the earth I
> may by my faith and works render all that aid in bearing up
> against and stemming the tide of wickedness, with which Satan
> seeks to sweep righteousness from the earth, which one bearing
> the Priesthood that the Lord has in his goodness bestowed upon
> me, should ever afford. My words are not sufficient to express
> what I hope and pray my actions and course of life will do, viz:
> my thankfulness and gratitude for the privileges and blessings I
> enjoy in being associated with those whom God has chosen and
> endowed with power to battle with Satan and to establish right-
> eousness and purity among men upon the earth.[1]

Perhaps George Q. Cannon's two most pronounced charac-
teristics were his gratitude to the Lord and his remarkable dedication to the Lord's work. Both of these traits are illustrated in
this quotation from his journal:

> While reflecting upon the goodness and condescension of the
> Lord to me, my heart was filled with joy and happiness unspeak-
> able and it seemed as though I could not contain a particle more
> without bursting. It was indeed a fulness. My tongue and lan-
> guage are far too feeble to express the feelings I experience when
> pondering upon the work of the Lord, and upon his love and
> kindness to me from my earliest childhood unto the present time.
> Oh, that my tongue and my time and talents and all that I have

or possess may be employed to his honor and glory, in glorifying His name and in spreading a knowledge of His attributes wherever my lot may be cast.[2]

Several references which Elder Cannon made indicate that he received the most sacred of all experiences—that of the visitation of the Lord Jesus Christ. This magnificent blessing occurred while he was still in his early twenties during his Hawaiian mission. Bryant S. Hinckley writes:

The men are few in the world's history who have been granted the glorious visitation given to George Q. Cannon in his young days on that far distant island. There he talked to the Lord as one man talks with another. Fifty years afterward when he visited the Islands, during their Jubilee Celebration, 1900, he was riding with Brother Wooley, touring the Islands. When he reached a certain place, he asked to get out, and he went alone into the garden where fifty years before, the God of Heaven appeared to him, then a lonely and humble missionary.[3]

Near the close of his fruitful life, President George Q. Cannon bore this powerful testimony of the Savior, a testimony which no doubt stemmed from the missionary experiences of his early years:

I know that Jesus lives, for I have seen him. I know that this is the Church of God and that it is founded on Jesus Christ, our Redeemer. I testify to you of these things as one who knows—as one of the Apostles of the Lord Jesus Christ that can bear witness to you today in the presence of the Lord that he lives and that he will live, and come to reign on the earth.[4]

NOTES

CHAPTER 1: INTRODUCTION

1. President Cannon, christened George Cannon, adopted his mother's maiden name, Quayle, as a middle name during the gold rush to avoid confusion with another George Cannon who was in California at the same time he was (*Church News*, January 14, 1967). His middle name will be used throughout this book to save confusion with his father, who was also named George Cannon.

2. *Denver Republican*, April 13, 1901.

3. *Deseret News 1991–1992 Church Almanac* (Salt Lake City: Deseret News Press, 1992), p. 41.

4. *Jubilee History of Latter-day Saint Sunday Schools* (Salt Lake City: Deseret Sunday School Union, 1900), p. 17.

5. *San Francisco Examiner*, April 12, 1901.

6. *Idaho Daily Statesman*, April 13, 1901.

7. *Des Moines Iowa Register*, April 14, 1901.

8. Heber J. Grant, "President George Q. Cannon," *The Young Women's Journal*, 12 (June, 1900), 243–45.

9. Bryant S. Hinckley, *The Faith of Our Pioneer Fathers* (Salt Lake City: Deseret Book Company, 1965), p. 175.

10. Orson F. Whitney, *History of Utah* (Salt Lake City: George Q. Cannon & Sons, 1892–1904), 4:663.

11. Mark W. Cannon, Address given at dedication of George Q. Cannon Center, Brigham Young University, Provo, Utah, November 10, 1958.

12. Beatrice Cannon Evans and Janath Russell Cannon, eds., *Cannon Family Historical Treasury* (Salt Lake City: Publishers Press, 1967), p. 113.

13. John Nicholson, cited by James H. Anderson, "President George Q. Cannon," *Lives of Our Leaders* (Salt Lake City: Deseret News, 1901), p. 33.

14. John D. Lee, *A Mormon Chronicle: The Diaries of John D. Lee*, Glass Cleleand and Juanita Brooks, eds. (San Marino Library, 1955), pp. 115–16.

15. Mark W. Cannon, "The Mormon Issue in Congress, 1872–1882, Drawing on the Experience of Territorial Delegate George Q. Cannon," Ph. D. dissertation, Harvard University, 1960.

16. *The Boston Globe*, April 13, 1901.

17. B. F. Cummings, Jr., "Shining Lights," *The Contributor*, 16 (December, 1894), 131.

18. George Q. Cannon, Address delivered at Salt Lake City, November 14, 1880, printed in *Journal of Discourses* (Liverpool, England, F. D. and S. W. Richards, 1854 ff), 23:135.

CHAPTER 2: THE PREPARATION

1. Parley P. Pratt, *Autobiography of Parley Parker Pratt* (Salt Lake City: Deseret Book Company, 1966), pp. 130–31.

2. Brigham H. Roberts, *The Life of John Taylor* (Salt Lake City: Bookcraft, Inc., 1963), p. 28.

3. Ibid., p. 29.

4. John Q. Cannon, *George Cannon: The Immigrant* (Salt Lake City, 1927), p. 91. Accounts differ as to whether this man's name was Mason or Bacon, and whether Leonora's friend was his daughter or his wife. See Andrew Jenson, *Latter-day Saint Biographical Encyclopedia* (Salt Lake City: Deseret News Press, 1901), 1:43.

5. Roberts, *Life of John Taylor*, p. 30.

6. Andrew Jenson, "George Q. Cannon," *Biographical Encyclopedia*, 1:14–15.

7. Doctrine & Covenants 118:6.

8. Pratt, *Autobiography*, pp. 130–31.

9. John Q. Cannon, *George Cannon: The Immigrant*, p. 94.

10. Joseph J. Cannon, "George Q. Cannon," *Instructor*, 79 (February, 1944), p. 67.

11. Anderson, *Lives of Our Leaders*, p. 35.

12. Marian Cannon Bennion, "Where the Cannon Family Came from and Why They Are in America," Address given at the Angus M. Cannon

Family Reunion, Salt Lake City, Utah, July 22, 1957.

13. Elizabeth Cannon Sauls, "The Life of George Q. Cannon" (Provo, Utah: pamphlet, 1956), p. 4.

14. Richard L. Evans, *A Century of "Mormonism" in Great Britain* (Salt Lake City: *Deseret News Press,* 1937), p. 96.

15. John Q. Cannon, *George Cannon: The Immigrant,* pp. 94–95.

16. Evans and Cannon, *Treasury,* p. 35.

17. Jenson, *Biographical Encyclopedia,* I:144.

18. Leonora Taylor, "Letter from Leonora Taylor to John Taylor," *Millennial Star,* I (July, 1840), 63–65.

19. Evans and Cannon, *Treasury,* p. 36.

20. Pratt, *Autobiography,* p. 301.

21. John Q. Cannon, *George Cannon: The Immigrant,* p. 97.

22. Evans and Cannon, *Treasury,* p. 161.

23. Joseph J. Cannon, "George Q. Cannon," *Instructor,* 79 (February, 1944), 73.

24. George Q. Cannon, "How I Obtained My Testimony of the Truth," *Young Women's Journal,* 4 (December 1892), 123.

25. E. L. Sloan, "Minutes of a Conference held in Bradford, Sunday, August 10, 1862," *Millennial Star,* 24 (September 6, 1862), 563.

26. George Q. Cannon, "How I Obtained My Testimony of the Truth," p. 123.

27. George Q. Cannon, Address to the Brigham Young Academy, Provo, Utah, April, 1899.

28. Evans and Cannon, *Treasury,* p. 38.

29. John Q. Cannon, *George Cannon: The Immigrant,* p. 105.

30. Evans and Cannon, *Treasury,* p. 87.

31. Joseph J. Cannon, "George Q. Cannon," *Instructor,* 79 (March, 1944), p. 117.

32. Evans and Cannon, *Treasury,* p. 40.

33. Ibid.

34. John Q. Cannon, *George Cannon: The Immigrant,* p. 145.

35. Evans and Cannon, *Treasury,* p. 46.

36. John Q. Cannon, *George Cannon: The Immigrant,* p. 101.

37. Sauls, *Life*, pp. 5–6.

38. John Q. Cannon, *George Cannon: The Immigrant*, p. 110.

39. Evans and Cannon, *Treasury*, p. 48.

40. Ibid., p. 51.

41. Ibid., p. 54.

42. Joseph J. Cannon, "George Q. Cannon," *Instructor*, 79 (March, 1944), p. 119.

43. George Q. Cannon, *The Life of Joseph Smith* (Salt Lake City: Deseret Book, 1986), p. 20.

44. George Q. Cannon, Semiannual Conference Address, Conference Reports, April, 1900, pp. 11–14.

45. Joseph J. Cannon, "George Q. Cannon," *Instructor*, 79 (April, 1944), 163.

46. Evans and Cannon, *Treasury*, p. 240.

47. John Q. Cannon, *George Cannon: The Immigrant*, p. 131.

48. George Q. Cannon, "Joseph Smith, the Prophet," *Juvenile Instructor*, 5 (October 29, 1870), 174–75.

49. Ibid., p. 158.

50. George Q. Cannon, "History of the Church," *Juvenile Instructor*, 6 (September 30, 1871), 158.

51. Evans and Cannon, *Treasury*, p. 63.

52. Ibid., p. 65.

53. John Q. Cannon, *George Cannon: The Immigrant*, p. 146.

54. George Q. Cannon, *My First Mission* (Salt Lake City: *Juvenile Instructor* Office, 1879), preface.

55. Joseph J. Cannon, "George Q. Cannon," *Instructor*, 79 (April, 1944), 161.

56. Jenson, "George Q. Cannon," *Biographical Encyclopedia*, 1:44.

57. Cannon, *My First Mission*, p. 9.

58. Roberts, *Life of John Taylor*, p. 169.

CHAPTER 3: THE GOLD MISSION

1. John R. Young, *Memoirs* (Salt Lake City: Deseret News Press, 1920), pp. 14–15.

2. George Q. Cannon, "History of the Church," *Juvenile Instructor*, 8 (July 6, 1872), 107.

3. Roberts, *Life of John Taylor*, p. 174.

4. Ibid., p. 183.

5. Thomas L. Kane, "Historical Address," cited in Roberts, *Life of John Taylor*, p. 172.

6. Roberts, *Life of John Taylor*, p. 185.

7. Joseph J. Cannon, "George Q. Cannon," *Instructor*, 79 (May, 1944), 209.

8. George Q. Cannon, "Topics of the Times," *Juvenile Instructor*, 18 (December 13, 1883), 377–78.

9. Ibid.

10. Roberts, *Life of John Taylor*, p. 190.

11. Ibid., p. 191–92.

12. Joseph J. Cannon, "George Q. Cannon," *Instructor*, 79 (May 1944), 210.

13. Evans and Cannon, *Treasury*, p. 118.

14. George Q. Cannon, "History of the Church," *Juvenile Instructor*, 8 (December 6, 1873), 195.

15. Ibid., 8 (December 20, 1873), 203.

16. Ibid., 8 (December 6, 1873), 195.

17. John Q. Cannon, *George Cannon: The Immigrant*, p. 147.

18. George Q. Cannon, "History of the Church," *Juvenile Instructor*, 19 (January 17, 1874), 22.

19. Ibid.

20. Orson F. Whitney, *Life of Heber C. Kimball* (Salt Lake City: Bookcraft, 1945), p. 390.

21. Brigham H. Roberts, *A Comprehensive History of The Church of Jesus Christ of Latter-day Saints* (Provo, Utah: Brigham Young University Press, 1965), 3:346–47.

22. Roberts, CH, 3: 349–51.

23. Ibid., 3:347.

24. Evans and Cannon, *Treasury*, p. 119.

25. George Q. Cannon, "Twenty Years Ago," *Juvenile Instructor*, 4 (January 16, 1869), 13.

26. George Q. Cannon, Personal journals, Church Historian's Office, Salt Lake City, Utah, October 19, 1849.

27. Ibid., October 29, 1849.

28. Leroy R. Hafen and Ann W. Hafen, *Journals of the Forty-Niners* (Glendale, California: The Arthur H. Clark Company, 1954), 2:141–272.

29. Cannon Journal, October 30, 1849. Brother Cannon's journal will be referred to hereafter as simply "Journal."

30. George Q. Cannon, "Twenty Years Ago," *Juvenile Instructor*, 4 (March 27, 1869), 52–53.

31. Ibid., 4 (April 10, 1869), 60.

32. Journal, November 11, 1848.

33. Ibid., Tuesday, November 13, 1849.

34. George Q. Cannon, "Twenty Years Ago," *Juvenile Instructor*, 4 (May 8, 1869), 78.

35. Hafen, *Forty-Niners*, 2:141–272.

36. George Q. Cannon, "Topics of the Times," *Juvenile Instructor*, 36 (December 15, 1883), 377–78.

37. Ibid.

38. Journal, Sunday, November 25, 1849.

39. George Q. Cannon, "Twenty Years Ago," *Juvenile Instructor*, 4 (June 5, 1869), 92.

40. Joseph J. Cannon, "George Q. Cannon," *Instructor*, 79 (July, 1944), 319.

41. George Q. Cannon, "Twenty Years Ago," *Juvenile Instructor*, 4 (January 16, 1869), 13–14.

42. Joseph J. Cannon, "George Q. Cannon," *Instructor*, 79 (August, 1944), 368.

43. Ibid.

44. John Q. Cannon, *George Cannon: The Immigrant*, p. 148.

45. Journal, October 8–15, 1850.

46. *Deseret News,* November 16, 1850, p. 155.

47. Ibid.

48. Journal, Tuesday, September 24, 1850.

49. "California Mission Journal History," Wednesday, September 25, 1850.

50. George Q. Cannon, *My First Mission,* preface.

51. Ibid.

CHAPTER 4: THE HAWAIIAN MISSION

1. "Journal History of The Church of Jesus Christ of Latter-day Saints," MS, Church Historian's Office, Salt Lake City, Utah, October 8, 1854 (See also *Deseret News,* 5:48).

2. Journal, October 18, 1850.

3. Journal History, September 25, 1850, p. 2.

4. "California Mission History," MS, Church Historian's Office, Salt Lake City, Utah, n. d.

5. George Q. Cannon, address delivered at Hooperville, Utah, June 27, 1881, *Journal of Discourses* (Liverpool, England: F. D. and S. W. Richards, 1854), 22:289.

6. Hinckley, *Faith,* p. 163.

7. Cannon, *My First Mission,* p. 15.

8. Ibid., p. 14.

9. Ibid., p. 12.

10. Ibid., p. 15.

11. Ibid., p. 17.

12. Kate B. Carter, *Treasures of Pioneer History* (Salt Lake City: Daughters of Utah Pioneers, 1956), 5:133. (Minutes of a meeting of the Twelve in Nauvoo, May 23, 1843).

13. Cannon, *My First Mission,* p. 17.

14. Journal, December 14, 1850.

15. Journal, December 25, 1850.

16. Journal, January 13, 1851.

17. Journal, January 18, 1851.

18. Cannon, *My First Mission*, p. 22.

19. Ibid., p. 27.

20. Ibid., p. 28.

21. Marba C. Josephson, "A Glance at Hawaiian Mission History," *Improvement Era*, 53 (August, 1950), 619–20.

22. Journal, February, 1851.

23. Ibid.

24. Hinckley, *Faith*, p. 165.

25. Andrew Jenson, compiler, Manuscript History of the Hawaiian Mission, Church Historian's Office, Salt Lake City, Utah.

26. Letter from Brigham Young, Salt Lake City, April 2, 1851, George Q. Cannon papers, Church Historian's Office.

27. William A. Cole and Elwin W. Jensen, *Israel in the Pacific* (Salt Lake City: Publishers Press, 1961), p. 386.

28. Cannon, *My First Mission*, p. 66.

29. Josephson, "A Glance," p. 620.

30. George Q. Cannon, letter to Leonora Taylor, Lahaina, Maui, S. I., August 22, 1851, reprinted in "The Sandwich Islands Mission," *Millennial Star*, 45 (September 11, 1852), 493.

31. Cannon, *My First Mission*, p. 47.

32. Cannon, Letter to Leonora Taylor, August 22, 1851.

33. William Perkins, Manuscript History of the Hawaiian Mission, January 19, 1852.

34. Cannon, Letter to Leonora Taylor, August 22, 1851.

35. Cannon, *My First Mission*, p. 69.

36. Ibid.

37. Journal, December 8, 1852.

38. Cannon, *My First Mission*, p. 69.

39. Ibid., p. 71.

40. Journal, December 24, 1853.

41. Excerpt from the Journal of Elder Karren, Manuscript History of the Hawaiian Mission, January 31, 1854.

42. George Q. Cannon, Letter to Brigham Young, Honolulu, Oahu, S. I.,

November 20, 1853, George Q. Cannon Papers, Church Historian's Office, Salt Lake City, Utah.

43. Josephson, "A Glance," p. 620.

44. Manuscript History of the Hawaiian Mission, August 17, 1851.

45. George Q. Cannon, Letter to Leonora Taylor, August 22, 1851.

46. Ibid.

47. George Q. Cannon, "Sandwich Islands," *Juvenile Instructor,* 10 (July 10, 1875), 159–60.

48. Benjamin E. Johnson, Manuscript History of the Hawaiian Mission, March 29, 1853 (see also *Millennial Star,* 15:428).

49. William E. Farrer, Manuscript History of the Hawaiian Mission, July 29, 1854.

50. Journal, March 19, 1851.

51. "Sandwich Islands," p. 160.

52. Ibid.

53. Journal, September 1, 1852.

54. Journal, April 5, 1852.

55. Ibid.

56. Journal, August 27, 1852.

57. Journal, March 8, 1851.

58. Ibid.

59. Journal, May 11, 1851.

60. Journal, December 12, 1851.

61. *Deseret News,* November 27, 1852 (see also Journal History, April 6, 1852, p. 9).

62. Joseph F. Smith, Address delivered at Salt Lake City, April 6, 1884, *Journal of Discourses* (Liverpool, England: F. D. and S. W. Richards, 1854), 25:100–1.

63. Cannon, *My First Mission,* pp. 33–34.

64. Journal, April 4, 1854.

65. George Q. Cannon, "Sandwich Islands," *Juvenile Instructor,* 10 (Saturday, August 7, 1875), 191–92.

66. Cannon, *My First Mission,* p. 43.

67. Journal, February 6, 1853.

68. George Q. Cannon, Letter, Wailuku, Maui, S. I., March 1, 1852, in "Intelligence from the Sandwich Islands," *Millennial Star,* 14 (October 2, 1852), 554–56.

69. Journal History, Tuesday, November 25, 1851, p. 1.

70. D. James Cannon, "Across the Years," in "Hawaiian Mission in Review; Ka Elele O Hawaii," pamphlet (Brigham Young University, Special Collections, Provo, Utah).

71. George Q. Cannon, Letter, November 25, 1851, in Journal History for that date, p. 1.

72. Journal, October 6, 1853.

73. Journal History, Tuesday, November 25, 1851, p. 1.

74. "Intelligence from the Sandwich Islands," p. 555.

75. Journal History, November 25, 1851, p. 1.

76. George Q. Cannon, "Missionary Sketches," *Juvenile Instructor,* 5 (Saturday, August 6, 1870), 123.

77. Joseph J. Cannon, "George Q. Cannon," *Instructor,* 79 (September, 1944), 418–19.

78. Journal, March 31, 1851.

79. Journal, June 25, 1852.

80. William J. Perkins, Letter to Brother Charles C. Rich, Lahaina, March 8, 1852, in Journal History for the same date, p. 2.

81. Journal, Sunday, October 10, 1852.

82. Cannon, *My First Mission,* p. 55.

83. Journal, February 7, 1853.

84. Ibid.

85. Journal, April 29, 1852.

86. B. F. Cummings, Jr., "Shining Lights," *Contributor,* 16 (December, 1884), 124.

87. Journal, May 30, 1852.

88. Journal, July 7, 1852.

89. Journal, March 23, 1853.

90. Joseph J. Cannon, "George Q. Cannon," *Instructor,* 79 (September 18, 1944), 422.

91. Cannon, *My First Mission,* p. 63.

92. Journal, December 11, 1852.

93. Journal, May 1, 1852.

94. Cannon, *My First Mission*, p. 65.

95. Journal, August 4, 1851.

96. Cannon, *My First Mission*, p. 64.

97. Journal, May 1, 1852.

98. George Q. Cannon, Letter, Wailuku, Maui, S. I., March 1, 1852 (George Q. Cannon Papers, Church Historian's Office, Salt Lake City, Utah).

99. Journal, April 20, 1854.

100. Journal, October 31, 1853.

101. Journal, April 4, 1854.

102. Journal, July 29, 1854.

103. Jenson, "George Q. Cannon," *Biographical Encyclopedia*, p. 45.

104. Cannon, *My First Mission*, p. 75.

CHAPTER 5: THE *WESTERN STANDARD* MISSION

1. Parley Parker Pratt, *Autobiography*, p. 409.

2. Jenson, "George Q. Cannon," *Biographical Encyclopedia*, p. 45.

3. Journal History of the Church (Church Historian's Office, Salt Lake City), November 28, 1854.

4. Jerreld L. Newquist, ed. *Gospel Truth* (Salt Lake City: Deseret Book, 1957), xv.

5. Joseph J. Cannon, "George Q. Cannon," *Instructor*, 79 (November, 1944), 510.

6. Joseph J. Cannon, "George Q. Cannon," *Instructor*, 79 (February, 1945), 57. The name of the firm is not mentioned, but was most likely the *Deseret News*. (See *Deseret News* 5:77.)

7. George Q. Cannon, *Writings from the "Western Standard"* (Liverpool: George Q. Cannon, 42, Islington, 1864), p. vi.

8. Jenson, "George Q. Cannon," *Biographical Encyclopedia*, p. 45.

9. *Deseret News*, 5:77. (See also Journal History, May 10, 1855, p. 1.)

10. George Q. Cannon, "Topics of the Times," p. 65.

11. Journal, May 21–22, 1855.

12. Elder Joseph Bull, Letter to James McKnight, June 27, 1855, printed in *Deseret News* 5:222. (See also Journal History, June 27, 1855, p. 2.)

13. George Q. Cannon, *Writings from the Western Standard*, p. vii.

14. Ibid.

15. Joseph J. Cannon, *Instructor*, 79 (November, 1944), p. 512.

16. Ibid.

17. Elizabeth Cannon Sauls, "The Life of George Q. Cannon" (pamphlet), Provo, Utah 1956, p. 12.

18. George Q. Cannon, Letter to Brigham Young, San Francisco, August 31, 1855 (George Q. Cannon Papers, Church Historian's Office, Salt Lake City, Utah).

19. Matthew F. Wilkie, Letter to Elder Joseph Cain, San Francisco, July 27, 1855, printed in *Deseret News* 5:222. (See also Journal History, July 27, 1855, p. 2.)

20. *Deseret News* 5:286. (See also Journal History, September 23, 1855, p. 5.)

21. George Q. Cannon, Letter to Brigham Young, San Francisco, January 26, 1856.

22. *Deseret News* 6:48. (See also Journal History, April 16, 1856, p. 2.)

23. *Deseret News* 6:40, Minutes of the General Conference in Hawaii. (See also Journal History, April 8, 1856, p. 1.)

24. George Q. Cannon, Letter to Brigham Young, San Francisco, January 26, 1856 (papers).

25. Evans and Cannon, *Treasury*, p. 92.

26. Ibid.

27. Matthew F. Wilkie, Letter, March 22, 1854, printed in *The Mormon*, May 16, 1854. (See Journal History, March 22, 1854, p. 7.)

28. George Q. Cannon, Letter to Brigham Young, San Francisco, August 31, 1855 (George Q. Cannon papers).

29. Ibid., May 26, 1856.

30. Matthew F. Wilkie, Letter March 22, 1854, printed in *The Mormon*, May 16, 1853.

31. George Q. Cannon, Letter to Brigham Young, March 1, 1854 (George Q. Cannon papers).

32. George Q. Cannon, *Writings from the Western Standard*, p. viii.

33. Roberts, *Comprehensive History*, 4:58.

34. George Q. Cannon, *Western Standard*, February 23, 1856.

35. George Q. Cannon, Letter to John Taylor, San Francisco, July 14, 1855. (See also Journal History, August 1, 1855, p. 3.)

36. *Deseret News* 5:286. (See also Journal History, September 23, 1855, p. 5.)

37. Ibid.

38. George Q. Cannon, *Writings from the Western Standard*, p. vii.

39. Joseph J. Cannon, *Instructor*, 79 (November, 1944), 513.

40. Prospectus of the *Western Standard*, San Francisco, California, January 4, 1856.

41. George Q. Cannon, *Writings from the "Western Standard,"* p. vii.

42. B. F. Cummings, Jr., "Shining Lights," *Contributor*, 16 (December, 1894), 127.

43. George Q. Cannon, *Writings from the "Western Standard"* p. vii.

44. *The Deseret Weekly*, 56:705. (See also Jerreld Newquist, "The Western Standard," *Improvement Era*, 62 [April, 1959], 238.)

45. Ibid.

46. George Q. Cannon, *Writings from the Western Standard*, p. 8.

47. *The Deseret Weekly*, 56:705.

48. Brigham Young, Address at Salt Lake City, August 31, 1856, *Journal of Discourses*, 4:36.

49. George Q. Cannon, *Western Standard*, February 23, 1856.

50. Ibid.

51. Deseret News 6:69. (See also Journal History, February 23, 1856, p. 1)

52. Reprinted in the *Western Standard*, March 1, 1856.

53. George Q. Cannon, Letter to Brigham Young, San Francisco, March 1, 1856 (papers).

54. George Q. Cannon, *Writings from the Western Standard*, p. iv.

55. George Q. Cannon, Letter to Brigham Young, October 31, 1856 (papers).

56. George Q. Cannon, *Western Standard*, November 15, 1856.

57. Joseph J. Cannon, "George Q. Cannon," *Instructor*, 79 (November, 1944), p. 513.

58. George Q. Cannon, Letter to Brigham Young, San Francisco, February 19, 1857 (papers).

59. George Q. Cannon, Letter to Brigham Young, December 3, 1855 (papers).

60. Ibid.

61. George Q. Cannon, *Western Standard*, February 23, 1856.

62. Ibid.

63. Fourteenth General Epistle of the Church, December, 1856. (Excerpt in Kate B. Carter, *Treasures of Pioneer History*, 1957, 6:14–15.)

64. George Q. Cannon, *Western Standard*, September 18, 1857.

65. George Q. Cannon, Letter to Brigham Young, August 31, 1857.

66. Ibid.

67. George Q. Cannon, *Western Standard*, January 24, 1857.

68. Ibid., May 3, 1856.

69. Ibid., December 13, 1856.

70. Ibid.

71. Ibid., December 6, 1856.

72. Ibid., December 20, 1856.

73. *Deseret News*, November 1, 1856.

74. Ibid., 7:174. (See also Journal History, July 24, 1857, p. 2.)

75. George Q. Cannon, *Western Standard*, January 10, 1857.

76. Ibid., November 29, 1856.

77. Ibid.

78. Ibid., January 10, 1857.

79. Ibid., September 18, 1857.

80. Jenson, *Biographical Encyclopedia*, p. 46.

81. Evans and Cannon, *Treasury*, p. 248.

82. William L. Knecht and Peter L.Crawley, eds., *History of Brigham Young, 1847–1867* (Berkeley, California: Mass Cal Associates, 1964), p. 218. (See also *Deseret News* 7:365 and Journal History, January 19, 1858, p. 2.)

83. Joseph J. Cannon, "George Q. Cannon," *Instructor*, 79 (November, 1944), p. 514.

84. George Q. Cannon, *Western Standard*, September 18, 1857.

CHAPTER 6: THE EASTERN STATES MISSION

1. Gustive O. Larson, *Outline History of Utah and the Mormons* (Salt Lake City: Deseret Book Company, 1958), p. 88.

2. Roberts, *Comprehensive History*, 4:298.

3. "Journal History of the Church," April 7, 1858, p. 1.

4. Wendell J. Ashton, *Voice in the West* (New York: Duel, Sloan & Pearce, 1950), pp. 375–76.

5. "Manuscript History of the Fillmore Ward" (Church Historian's Office, Salt Lake City, Utah), p. 12.

6. Jenson, *Biographical Encyclopedia*, p. 46.

7. *Deseret News*, August 18, 1858, 108.

8. Ibid. (See also Ashton, *Voice in the West*, p. 92.)

9. Evans and Cannon, *Treasury*, p. 123.

10. Ashton, *Voice in the West*, p. 89.

11. Evans and Cannon, *Treasury*, p. 124–25.

12. Joseph J. Cannon, "George Q. Cannon," *Instructor*, 79 (December, 1944), 576.

13. Cannon and Evans, *Treasury*, p. 125.

14. Larson, *Outline History*, p. 89.

15. *Deseret News*, July 14, 1858, p. 96.

16. George Q. Cannon, "Fragments," *Juvenile Instructor*, 28 (April 15, 1893), 220.

17. John Q. Cannon, *George Q. Cannon: The Immigrant*, p. 150.

18. George Q. Cannon, "Fragments," 220.

19. Joseph J. Cannon, "George Q. Cannon," *Instructor*, 79 (December, 1944), 577.

20. Hinckley, *Faith*, p. 171.

21. Ibid.

22. Jenson, *Biographical Encyclopedia*, p. 47.

23. Anderson, *Lives of Our Leaders*, p. 39.

24. Journal History, August 29, 1858, p. 1. (See also "Manuscript History of Brigham Young," 1858, p. 951.)

25. Albert L. Zobell, Jr., *Sentinel in the East* (Salt Lake City: Nicholas G. Morgan, Sr., 1965), p. xii. (See also Journal of Wilford Woodruff, February 25, 1858, and Roberts, *Comprehensive History of the Church*, 4:346, which will be abbreviated CHC hereafter).

26. George Q. Cannon, Letter to Brigham Young, Philadelphia, Pa., April 14, 1859 (George Q. Cannon Papers, Church Historian's Office, Salt Lake City).

27. Ibid., April 14, 1859 (papers).

28. Ibid.

29. Ibid., Washington City, January 26, 1859 (papers).

30. Ibid., April 14, 1859 (papers).

31. Ibid., St. Louis, Missouri, March 4, 1859 (papers).

32. Robert B. Day, *They Made Mormon History* (Salt Lake City: Deseret Book Co., 1968), pp. 143–44. (See also Zobell, *Sentinel in the East*, p. 207).

33. George Q. Cannon, Letter to Brigham Young, New York City, July, 1859 (papers).

34. Matthias Cowley, *Prophets and Patriarchs* (Chattanooga, Tennessee: Ben E. Rich, 1902), p. 156.

35. Roberts, CHC, 4:500.

36. George Q. Cannon, Letter to Brigham Young, Washington City, January 18, 1860 (papers).

37. Ibid., Philadelphia, March 18, 1859 (papers).

38. Ibid., April 14, 1859.

39. Ibid.

40. Hubert Howe Bancroft, *History of Utah* (Salt Lake City: Bookcraft, 1964), pp. 592, 623.

41. George Q. Cannon, Letter to Brigham Young, Washington City, March 26, 1860 (papers).

42. Ibid., St. Louis, April 23, 1859 (papers).

43. Ibid., Washington City, March 26, 1860.

44. Zobell, *Sentinel in the East*, p. 174.

45. Roberts, CHC, 4:355–56.

46. The following incident illustrates Governor Cumming's determination to protect the citizens of Utah from violence and injustice. Some of the

officers in Johnston's army trumped up a charge of counterfeiting against Brigham Young and proposed to use military force to arrest him, i. e., surround his home, use artillery to "make a breach in the wall," seize him and carry him back to Army Headquarters at Camp Floyd. Hoping to get Governor Cumming's sanction, they laid the details of this diabolical plan before him. He answered them, "When you have a right to take Brigham Young, gentlemen, you shall have him without creeping through walls. You shall enter by his door with heads erect as becomes representatives of your government. But till that time, gentlemen, you can't touch Brigham Young while I live, by God" (Bancroft, p. 573).

47. Zobell, *Sentinel in the East,* p. 175.

48. Ibid.

49. Journal History, August 19, 1860, p. 4.

50. George Q. Cannon, "Editorial Thoughts," *Juvenile Instructor,* 19 (January 15, 1884), 24–25.

51. Roberts, CHC, 5:500.

52. "Manuscript History of the Eastern States Mission"(Church Historian's Office, Salt Lake City), March 9, 1858.

53. Doctrine & Covenants 33:6–7.

54. Ibid., 45:71.

55. George Q. Cannon, Address, Tabernacle, Salt Lake City, Sunday, July 15, 1883, *Journal of Discourses,* 24:184–85.

56. Ibid.

57. William Mulder, *The Mormons in American History* (Salt Lake City: Extension Division, University of Utah, 1957), p. 18.

58. Robert B. Day, *They Made Mormon History,* p. 117 (See also *Millennial Star,* 18 [January 26, 1856] 52–54.)

59. Ibid.

60. William E. Berrett and Alma P. Burton, *Readings in L.D.S. Church History* (Salt Lake City: Deseret Book Co., 1965), 2:404.

61. Larson, *Outline History,* p. 93.

62. James Stephens Brown, *Life of Pioneer* (Salt Lake City: Cannon and Sons, 1900), p. 121.

63. Brigham Young, Heber C. Kimball, Willard Richards, "Sixth General

Epistle of the Presidency of the Church," *Millennial Star*, 14 (January 15, 1852), 23.

64. George Q. Cannon, *Western Standard*, March 22, 1856.

65. Day, *Mormon History*, p. 123.

66. Brigham Young, Heber C. Kimball, Jedediah M. Grant, "Thirteenth General Epistle," *Millennial Star*, 14 (January 26, 1856), 54.

67. George Q. Cannon, Letter to Brigham Young, St. Joseph, Missouri, June 28, 1860 (papers).

68. Ibid., New York, July 22, 1859.

69. Andrew Love Neff, *History of Utah: 1847 to 1869* (Salt Lake City: Deseret News Press, 1940), p. 595.

70. Journal History, April 23, 1860, p. 1.

71. Ibid., October 23, 1859, p. 3.

72. Brigham Young, Heber C. Kimball, Willard Richards, "Seventh General Epistle of the Presidency of the Church," *Millennial Star*, 14 (July 17, 1852), 325.

73. Kate B. Carter, *Treasures of Pioneer History* (Salt Lake City: Daughters of Utah Pioneers, 1956), 5:292.

74. Neff, *History of Utah*, pp. 579—580.

75. George Q. Cannon, Letter to Brigham Young, Washington, January 18, 1860 (papers).

76. Ibid.

77. Day, *Mormon History*, p. 133.

78. Larson, *Outline History*, p. 107.

79. Ibid.

80. Joseph J. Cannon, 79 (December, 1944), p. 578.

81. Preston Nibley, *Brigham Young: The Man and His Work* (Salt Lake City: Deseret Book Company, 1936), p. 352.

82. George Q. Cannon, Letter to Brigham Young, Washington, December 13, 1859 (papers).

83. Ibid., Letter to John Taylor, Washington City, March 30, 1860.

84. George Q. Cannon, Address at a meeting paying tribute to President Snow, B. Y. Academy, Provo, Utah, April 2, 1899 (filed in Brigham Young University Archives, Provo, Utah).

85. George Q. Cannon, *Deseret Weekly*, 40 (February 23, 1890), 377. (See also Jerreld Newquist, *Gospel Truth: Discourses and Writings of President George Q. Cannon* [Salt Lake City: Zion's Book Store, 1957], p. 213).

86. Brigham Young, Conference Address, April, 1860, In *Journal of Discourses*, 7:228.

87. Amasa M. Lyman and Charles C. Rich, Letter, Florence, Nebraska, June 13, 1860 (in "Journal History of the Church" for that date).

88. Joseph J. Cannon, "George Q. Cannon," *Instructor*, 79 (December, 1944), 578.

89. Blessing to apostleship, August 25, 1860, 5:00 p.m. (George Q. Cannon Papers, Church Historian's Office, Salt Lake City).

CHAPTER 7: THE EUROPEAN MISSION

1. Joseph J. Cannon, "George Q. Cannon," *Instructor*, 80 (January, 1945), 10.

2. Roberts, *CHC*, 5:83.

3. "British Mission Manuscript History," Saturday, August 18, 1860 (in Church Historian's Office, Salt Lake City).

4. Roberts, CHC, 5:83.

5. Brigham Young, Blessing of Apostleship upon George Q. Cannon, Church Historian's Office, August 25, 1860, 5:00 p.m. (in George Q. Cannon Papers, Church Historian's Office, Salt Lake City).

6. George Q. Smith, G. S. L. C., Utah, September 27, 1860, Journal History for that date, p. 1.

7. George Q. Cannon, Letter to Bros. Lyman and Rich, Florence, Nebraska Territory, November Territory, November 10, 1860 (Papers).

8. "British Mission Manuscript History," December 21, 1860, p. 1.

9. Roberts, CHC, 5:81–82, 96.

10. Richard L. Evans, *A Century of "Mormonism" in Great Britain* (Salt Lake City: The Deseret News Press, 1937), pp. 244–245.

11. George Q. Cannon, Letter to Brigham Young, Liverpool, January 3, 1861 (Papers).

12. George Q. Cannon, Letter to Brigham Young, Liverpool, January 18,

1861. All subsequent letters from Brother Cannon are to Brigham Young from Liverpool and contained in the Church Historian's Office unless otherwise marked.

13. George Q. Cannon, Letter, January 18, 1861.

14. George Q. Cannon, Letter, January 18, 1861.

15. Ibid., June 15, 1861.

16. See Doctrine & Covenants 87.

17. George Q. Cannon, Letter, June 15, 1861.

18. Brigham Young, Letter to George Q. Cannon, Salt Lake City, May 2, 1861, printed in *Millennial Star* 23:394 (See also Journal History of the Church for that date, p. 1).

19. Richard Vetterli, *Mormonism, Americanism and Politics* (Salt Lake City: Ensign Publishing Company, 1961), p. 237.

20. George Q. Cannon, "Topics of the Times," *Juvenile Instructor,* 17 (December 15, 1883), 378.

21. Ibid.

22. "Prospectus," *Millennial Star,* I (May, 1840), 1.

23. *Deseret News* 11:8. (See also Journal History, February 25, 1861, p. 2.)

24. George C. Lambert, "The Millennial Star," *Contributor,* 5 (March, 1884), 209–11.

25. Roberts, *CHC,* 5:86.

26. George Q. Cannon, Letter, May 31, 1861.

27. Ibid.

28. George Q. Cannon, Letter, May 31, 1861.

29. Ibid., March 31, 1861.

30. Ibid., September 7, 1861.

31. Ibid., February 9, 1864.

32. George Q. Cannon, *Writings from the "Western Standard"* (Liverpool: George Q. Cannon, 42, Islington, 1864), pp. iii-iv.

33. George Q. Cannon, Letter, December 12, 1862.

34. Ibid.

35. George Q. Cannon, "Editorial," *Millennial Star,* 24 (February 15, 1862), 106–7.

36. Ibid., 26 (June 4, 1863), 361.

37. Ibid., 26 (May 28, 1863), 346.

38. Ibid., 25 (October 4, 1863), 721–22.

39. George Q. Cannon, Address delivered at the Assembly Hall, Salt Lake City, Sunday, November 14, 1880, *Journal of Discourses*, 23:134.

40. Ibid., Sunday, November 23, 1884, *Journal of Discourses*, 26:282.

41. Anderson, "President George Q. Cannon," *Lives of Our Leaders* (Salt Lake City: *Deseret News Press*, 1901), p. 30.

42. George Q. Cannon, "Early Experiences in Preaching," *Juvenile Instructor*, 12 (February 15, 1877), 48.

43. Ibid.

44. Journal History, December 31, 1862, pp. 3–4.

45. Ibid.

46. George Q. Cannon, Letter, February 23, 1861.

47. Ibid., December 13, 1862.

48. Ibid., February 28, 1861.

49. Ibid., December 12, 1862.

50. Ibid.

51. Ibid., October 24, 1863.

52. Ibid., November 12, 1862.

53. Ibid., December 21, 1861.

54. Ibid.

55. Ibid., January 2, 1863.

56. Ibid., January 3, 1861.

57. George Q. Cannon, Letter to Heber C. Kimball, Liverpool, January 10, 1863 (Papers).

58. Joseph F. Smith, Letter to President Cannon, "British Mission Manuscript," February 5, 1861.

59. George Q. Cannon, Letter, February 28, 1861.

60. Joseph Bull, Letter to President Cannon, December 11, 1863 (in *Millennial Star* 26:29).

61. George Q. Cannon, Letter, December 7, 1863.

62. Ibid., January 26, 1864.

63. Andrew Jenson, *Biographical Encyclopedia*, p. 48.

64. George Q. Cannon, Letter, September 1, 1862.

65. Joseph Fielding Smith, *Life of Joseph F. Smith* (Salt Lake City: *Deseret News Press,* 1938), pp. 203–4.

66. George Q. Cannon, Letter, September 28, 1863.

67. George Q. Cannon, Letter, Geneva, Switzerland, October 11, 1862.

68. George Q. Cannon, Letter to Heber C. Kimball, January 10, 1863.

69. George Q. Cannon, Letter, April 17, 1863.

70. George Q. Cannon, Letter to the Quorum of Twelve, December 13, 1862.

71. George Q. Cannon, Letter, December 7, 1863.

72. George Q. Cannon, Letter to the Quorum of Twelve, February 27, 1863.

73. Ibid.

74. Ibid.

75. George Q. Cannon, Letter to Heber C. Kimball, January 10, 1863.

76. Ibid.

77. George Q. Cannon, Letter to the Quorum of Twelve, February 27, 1863.

78. Ibid.

79. Ibid.

80. Ibid.

81. "British Mission Manuscript History," May 21, 1861, p. 1.

82. George Q. Cannon, Letter, December 12, 1862.

83. George Q. Cannon, Letter to Heber C. Kimball, January 10, 1863.

84. George Q. Cannon, Letter, January 23, 1863.

85. Roberts, CHC, 5: 4.

86. Ibid.

87. George Q. Cannon, Letter, April 26, 1862.

88. *Deseret News* 11:340. (See also Journal History, April 16, 1862, p. 2.)

89. *Deseret News* 12:233. (See also Journal History, January 19, 1863, p. 2.)

90. *Deseret News* 11: 349. (See also Journal History, April 26, 1862, p. 1.)

91. George C. Lambert, "The Millennial Star," p. 210.

92. George Q. Cannon, Letter, May 10, 1862.

93. Ibid., Philadelphia, Pa., July 13, 1862.

94. Ibid., Washington, July 2, 1862.

95. Gustive O. Larson, *Outline History*, p. 87.

96. *Deseret News* 12: 233. (See Journal History, January 19, 1863, p. 2.)

97. Neff, *History of Utah*, p. 676.

98. Jenson, *Biographical Encyclopedia*, p. 47.

99. George Q. Cannon, Letter, Copenhagen, September 18, 1862.

100. Ibid., December 4, 1863.

101. George Q. Cannon, Letter to Elder Amasa M. Lyman, Liverpool, February 19, 1863.

102. George Q. Cannon, Letter to Heber C. Kimball, Liverpool, January 10, 1863.

103. George Q. Cannon, Letter, February 28, 1863.

104. Evans and Cannon, *Treasury*, p. 122.

105. Joseph Fielding Smith, *Life of Joseph F. Smith*, p. 204.

106. Joseph J. Cannon, "George Q. Cannon," *Instructor*, 80 (January, 1945), 13–14.

107. Evans, *Century of "Mormonism,"* p. 245.

108. Brigham Young, Heber C. Kimball, Jedediah M. Grant, "Thirteenth General Epistle," *Millennial Star*, 18 (January 26, 1856), 49–55.

109. Larson, *Outline History*, pp. 110–12.

110. "British Mission Manuscript History," April 16, 1861, April 23, 1861, May 16, 1861, etc.

111. "British Mission Manuscript History," January 5, 1861, p. 2.

112. Gustive O. Larson, "Some Remarkable Influence," *Millennial Star*, 98 (December 10, 1936), 789–90.

113. Larson, *Outline History*, p. 99.

114. George Q. Cannon, Letter, April 19, 1864.

115. Ibid., May 5, 1864.

116. Ibid., May 23, 1863.

117. Ibid., December 7, 1861.

118. Ibid.

119. Ibid., November 23, 1861.

120. Joseph J. Cannon, "George Q. Cannon," *Instructor*, 80 (January, 1945), p. 12.

121. George Q. Cannon. Letter, January 2, 1863.

122. Ibid., December 7, 1861.

123. Ibid.

124. Ibid., May 3, 1862.

125. Ibid., February 9, 1864.

126. Ibid., November 23, 1861.

127. Ibid., July 2, 1864.

128. Ibid., January 17, 1861.

129. Journal History, December 31, 1863, p. 2.

130. N. V. Jones, Letter to George Q. Cannon, May 21, 1861, printed in *Millennial Star* 23:396. (See also Journal History, May 21, 1861, p. 1.)

131. George Q. Cannon, Letter, May 3, 1862.

132. Ibid., June 27, 1863.

133. Journal History, December 31, 1863, p. 2.

134. George Q. Cannon, Letter, May 2, 1864.

135. Ibid., April 4, 1862.

136. Ibid., October 4, 1861.

137. Ibid.

138. *Millennial Star* 23:395. (See also Journal History, May 25, 1861, p. 1.)

139. Ibid., 24:588. (See also Journal History, July 17, 1862, p. 1.)

140. Joseph W. Young, Letter to George Q. Cannon, Great Salt Lake City, Utah Territory, January 17, 1863, printed in *Millennial Star* 25:157. (See also Journal History, January 17, 1863, p. 2.)

141. Ibid.

142. Larson, *Outline History*, p. 99.

143. Ibid.

144. Robert B. Day, *They Made Mormon History* (Salt Lake City: Deseret Book Company, 1968), p. 117.

145. Kate B. Carter, *Our Pioneer Heritage* (Salt Lake City: Daughters of Utah Pioneers, 1964), 7:48.

146. Ibid. 9:290.

147. "British Mission Manuscript History," February 16, 1861, p. 1.

148. Carter, *Our Pioneer Heritage*, 1:159.

149. Ibid., 7:48.

150. Gustive O. Larson, *Prelude to the Kingdom* (Francestown, New Hampshire: Marshall Jones Company, 1947), p. 100. (See also Day, *They Made Mormon History*, p. 120.)

151. Larson, *Prelude to the Kingdom*, pp. 139–40.

152. George Q. Cannon, Letter, June 7, 1863.

153. Ibid.

154. Ibid.

155. Charles Dickens, *The Uncommercial Traveler* (London: J. M. Dent & Co., n. d.), p. 222.

156. Ibid., p. 230.

157. Ibid., p. 221.

158. Ibid.

159. Ibid., p. 222.

160. Ibid., p. 223.

161. Ibid.

162. Ibid.

163. Ibid., p. 230.

164. Ibid., p. 230.

165. W. Bramall, E. L. Sloan, and Richard Palmer, Letter to George Q. Cannon, New York, July 19, 1863, printed in *Millennial Star*, 25:541. (See also Journal History for that date, p. 4.)

166. George Q. Cannon, Letter, November 1, 1863.

167. Ibid., December 7, 1863.

168. Jenson, *Biographical Encyclopedia*, p. 48.

169. Journal History, October 23, 1864, p. 3.

170. George Q. Cannon, Letter, February 28, 1863.

171. Ibid., May 23, 1864.

172. George Q. Cannon, "Valedictory," *Millennial Star*, 25:569. (See also Journal History, September 3, 1864, p. 1.)

173. Ibid.

174. *Millennial Star*, 25:569.

175. "British Mission Manuscript History," September 3, 1864, pp. 3–4.

176. George Q. Cannon, Letter to Pres. Daniel Wells and Brigham Young, Jr., September 18, 1864, printed in *Millennial Star,* 26:668. (See also Journal History for that date, p. 1.)

177. George Q. Cannon, Letter to British Mission, *Millennial Star,* 27:77. (See also Journal History, December 7, 1864, p. 2.)

178. Ibid.

CHAPTER 8: CONCLUSION

1. George Q. Cannon, Letter to Brigham Young, November 12, 1862 (Papers).

2. Journal, November 29, 1852.

3. Bryant S. Hinckley, *Faith,* p. 163.

4. J. E. Cardon and Samuel O. Bennion, *Testimonies of The Divinity of The Church of Jesus Christ of Latter-day Saints* (Independence, Missouri: Zion's Publishing Company, 1930), p. 87. The original source for this testimony is the *Deseret Weekly* 5:610. Another witness to President Cannon's testimony of this experience was Reddick N. Allred, who knew Brother Cannon personally: " . . . he told me that he knew that Jesus lived for he had seen him." This excerpt from Brother Allred's diary entry of April 12, 1901 is printed in Kate B. Carter, *Treasures of Pioneer History* (Salt Lake City: Daughters of Utah Pioneers, 1956), 5:369.

PHOTO CREDITS

Photos on pages 1, 91, and 124 appear courtesy of LDS Historical Department, Archives.

Photos on pages 7, 53, 90, 125, 210, and 211 appear courtesy of Richard Neitzel Holzapfel.

Index

as European Mission president,
162-63, 168-82
experiences success in Hawaii, 81-
87, 212-13
as First Counselor, 10, 25
foresaw future calling, 154
on the gathering, 144-45, 147-48
in the gold fields, 48-50, 113-14
gratitude and dedication of, 212
Hawaiian hardships of, 74-81
Hawaiian legacy of, 87-90
Hawaiian name of, 89
helps Parley P. Pratt, 91-94
immigrates to Nauvoo, Ill., 15-19
on John Taylor, 25
on Joseph Smith, 20-21
on journals of the Elders, 5-6
journeys to California, 40-48
learns Hawaiian, 64-66, 82
learns publishing trade, 25, 91-94
leaves Nauvoo, 30
lobbies in Washington, D.C., 139-
43, 183-87
meets Elizabeth Hoagland, 34
meets Joseph Smith, 20
meets Parley P. Pratt, 13
meets with Abraham Lincoln, 186
as a mission president, 112-13
and the Mormon Battalion, 31
narrowly escapes drowning, 132-33
ordained an Elder and a Seventy, 26
on poi, 75
and politics, 3, 139-43, 162
on poor persons, 151
prepares for Hawaiian Mission, 53-
56
pronounces blessing on European
Saints, 208
prophesies about California Saints,
106-7
prophesies to emigrants, 150
as a public speaker, 4, 83-84
publishes the *Deseret News*, 126-27
publishes the Hawaiian Book of
Mormon, 97-99, 102, 107

publishes the *Millennial Star*, 159,
163-68
publishes the *Western Standard*, 103-21
returns from European Mission,
206-10
returns from Hawaii, 91-93
returns to England, 187-89
sends money to Brigham Young, 100
serves in Hawaii, 57-64
on spiritual gifts, 14-15
spiritual gifts of, 84-86
spiritual manifestation of, 62, 111-
12, 213
spiritual nature of, 14
statements on the death of, 1, 2-5
suggests Church wagon trains, 151-
52
and Sunday School, 4
teaches the Hawaiians, 68-74
testimony of, 14, 213
and Thomas L. Kane, 31
toured European Mission, 176
on the trail west, 32-34
translates Book of Mormon into
Hawaiian, 66-68
for U.S. Senate, 184
visions of, 54-55, 62, 77, 86-87,
106-7, 111-12, 150, 154
visits relatives in England, 169
voyages to Hawaiian Islands, 55-57
wanted to be a missionary, 15, 154
in Washington D.C., 133-56
and *Western Standard* staff, 91 (photo)
on the "whittling and whistling"
brigade, 23-24
Cannon, George Quayle Jr. (son of
GQC), 111
Cannon, Georgiana Hoagland, 188,
189
Cannon, John Quayle, 11, 111, 122,
125, 129, 131, 132, 158
Cannon, Leonora (sister of GQC), 18,
24
Cannon, Mary Alice. *See* Lambert, Mary
Alice Cannon